sundance
a festival virgin's guide

surviving and thriving in park city at america's
most important film festival

1st edition

benjamin craig

illustrations by lee tatham

cinemagine media publishing
london

Sundance — A Festival Virgin's Guide
Surviving and Thriving in Park City at America's Most Important Film Festival.

Disclaimer
This publication is presented "as is," without warranty of any kind. Whilst every effort has been made to maintain the accuracy of information provided, the author, contributors, and/or the publisher cannot accept any liability whatsoever for incorrect or outdated information contained within. Furthermore, certain information presented in this publication may be based on the opinions and experiences of the author and/ or contributors and therefore should not be used in place of appropriate professional advice.

The views expressed in this publication are those of the author and/or contributors only and do not necessarily reflect those held by the Sundance Institute.

Trademarks
Certain words or phrases within this publication may be trademarks owned by third-party organisations. Although used without permission, trademarks are noted as such wherever possible. Any reference to trademarks within this publication is made solely for informational purposes and should in no way be considered a challenge to their ownership.

"Sundance — A Festival Virgin's Guide" and "Festival Virgin's Guide" are trademarks owned by Cinemagine Media Limited.

Published By
Cinemagine Media Publishing
3 Castelnau Row, London SW13 9EE, United Kingdom.
www.cinemagine.com
A division of Cinemagine Media Limited

2004 (1st edition)

ISBN 0-9541737-2-4

Printed in the United Kingdom.

Cover art by Lee Tatham
Book design by Benjamin Craig

Enquires for sales and distribution, textbook adoption, advertising, foreign language translation, editorial, and rights permissions concerning this book should be addressed to the publisher.

Visit Sundance — A Festival Virgin's Guide online
www.sundanceguide.net

preface and acknowledgments

Welcome to the second book in the *Festival Virgin's Guide* series. Little did I know that a bunch of notes made out of frustration during my first visit to the Cannes Film Festival many years ago would blossom into a series of books aimed at helping other festivalgoers avoid some of my negative experiences. Sundance is of course a very different beast to the famous French festival and brings a completely different set of challenges for the first-time visitor. Hopefully this book will help you meet these challenges and ensure that your experiences at the Sundance Film Festival are both successful and stress free.

Of course, an undertaking such as *Sundance — A Festival Virgin's Guide* could never be completed in isolation. I'm indebted to a group of wonderful people who have helped make this book a reality; paramount amongst them are those at the Sundance Institute, who not only gave me their blessing to write this book, but provided invaluable help and support for someone who was ultimately an independent writer. Special thanks must therefore go to a number of key Sundance Institute staff, and also to former staffers Courtney Stern and Nikki Lowry.

Also deserving of my sincerest thanks are the group of Sundance veterans who very kindly made available a slice of their valuable time to provide their own insights into all that is the Sundance Film Festival: Arianna Bocco, Linda Brown-Salomone, Tina Gharavi, Gary Hamilton, Eugene Hernandez, Andrew Herwitz, Charlotte Mickie, Mark Pogachefsky, Tiffany Shlain, and Jeremy Wooding. Finally, the following people have been instrumental in developing this book by providing a whole range of advice and support: David Martus, Stephena Runyan, Michelle Turner; my editor Barbara Bannon, and naturally, Lee Tatham, who created the wonderful cover artwork and map illustrations.

I hope you find this book useful, and I wish you all the best with your adventures in Park City at America's most important film festival.

Benjamin Craig
London
February 2004

table of contents

Part 4 — The Lowdown

Appendices

SUNDANCE - A FESTIVAL VIRGIN'S GUIDE

1ST EDITION

introduction

Much has been written about the Sundance Film Festival — some of it true, some of it more fanciful — and a fair number of myths have circulated around the event during its quarter-century history. The Sundance that many people are familiar with is perhaps one of idealistic independent filmmakers, hyperactive publicity, corporate invasions, and mind-boggling acquisition deals. But behind this façade is a genuine film festival that continues to offer unwavering support for independent filmmaking and, amongst all the successes of the past 25 years, has managed to retain an intimacy rarely found at other events of similar stature around the world. Sundance feels like a real film festival — where films, filmmakers, and the audience are the primary concern.

For most Sundance virgins, a big part of attending the festival for the first time is getting behind the myths and discovering this true Sundance, but the astronomical growth the event has experienced in recent years brings with it a set of unique challenges for the uninitiated. Sundance virgins need to contend not only with the altitude and what can simply be described as serious snow, but also with the fact that the festival takes place in a town which is reasonably spread out, geared primarily toward people on ski holidays, and disproportionately small in relation to the size of the event it hosts. So where do you start? How do you get to the festival, and where do you find that essential information that will make your visit fun, successful, and most importantly, stress free?

Sundance — A Festival Virgin's Guide is for independent filmmakers, film-industry professionals, and festivalgoers who are interested in gaining a deeper understanding of the event, how it operates, and how to make the most of their time in Park City. The book is intended to demystify the town and the festival, and to help make a visit both successful and enjoyable. Information in the guidebook is grouped broadly into four main sections:

The City — getting to Park City, getting around, places to stay, places to eat, and general information;

The Festival — its structure, how to attend, parties and hanging out, and all about the screenings;

The Biz — an overview of how the business side of the festival operates and some advice for filmmakers who are planning to head to Park City with a project in tow;

The Lowdown — a series of interviews with a selection of Sundance veterans from across the film industry.

In addition to these sections, a collection of appendices contains a wealth of additional information.

But before we move forward, please take a moment to glance over the following notes and bear them in mind as you read through this book.

Official Venues

During each festival, a group of official venues run by Sundance house a range of activities. Whilst the venues themselves remain fairly consistent from year to year, the festival is constantly reviewing and fine-tuning the event, and consequently, the locations of these venues may change. It's therefore always worth checking the Sundance film guide or festival Web site for any alterations to venue locations.

Prices

Currency exchange rates are in constant flux, but local prices change much more slowly over time. Consequently, all prices in this guide appear in local currency—in this case, U.S. dollars. For most Sundancers, this will probably be your own currency; however, for international visitors, more information on currencies and money in the United States can be found in the chapter entitled *Money* in section one of this book.

Phone Numbers

All phone numbers in this book include the full area code and local number. To call these numbers locally (from within the same area code), you can normally just dial the local number. Long-distance calls within the U.S. and Canada usually require you to dial 1 before the area code and local number. If you're calling from overseas, before dialling the area code and local number, you must dial your phone company's international direct number (often 00) and the country code for the U.S.A. (1).

And Finally...

It's worth remembering that whilst this book contains a large amount of information about Park City and the festival, it is by no means 100 percent comprehensive. As time passes, recommendations change; old places close while new places open, and some suggestions may not suit all tastes. Part of the fun of attending an event like Sundance for the first time is building your own library of experiences and anecdotes and scouting out new places that you can recommend to future Sundance virgins.

sundance — what's in a name?

Many can be forgiven for wondering just where in America they will find the town of Sundance, for surely that is the place which hosts this film festival they've heard so much about. Whilst there is actually a town called Sundance (in Wyoming), it doesn't host a famous film festival. "Sundance" is of course the banner under which Robert Redford runs many of his businesses and other initiatives, and although the festival is often referred to simply as "Sundance," the name is interchangeable with a whole community of organisations:

Sundance Institute

The Sundance Institute, a non-profit organisation, was founded by Robert Redford and is dedicated to the development of artists of independent vision and the exhibition of their new work. In 1981, Redford gathered a group of colleagues and friends at Sundance, Utah, to discuss new ways to enhance the artistic vitality of American film. Since that beginning almost a quarter of a century ago, the Sundance Institute has expanded its scope to include a range of programs that reflect the original mission of nurturing developing artists in a variety of disciplines and encouraging the independent spirit in both artists and their projects. www.sundance.org

Sundance Channel

Under the creative direction of Robert Redford, Sundance Channel brings television viewers daring and engaging feature films, shorts, documentaries, world cinema, and animation, shown uncut and with no commercials. Through its original programs, Sundance Channel connects viewers with filmmakers, the creative process, and the world of independent film. Launched in 1996, Sundance Channel is a venture between Robert Redford, Showtime Networks Inc., and Universal Studios. Sundance Channel operates independently of the non-profit Sundance Institute and the Sundance Film Festival, but shares the overall Sundance mission of supporting independent artists and providing them with wider opportunities to present their work to audiences. www.sundancechannel.com

Sundance Resort

In 1969, Robert Redford purchased land at the base of 12,000-foot Mount Timpanogos in Utah's Wasatch Mountains. This pristine place of natural beauty has become the Sundance Resort. The goal of the Sundance Resort is to offer a community for art and nature that will foster artistic pursuits and recreational activity while preserving the naturally beautiful and unique environment of Sundance. Sundance is an arts community, a recreational community, a community of people who appreciate the beauty of nature — and feel the responsibility to preserve it. www.sundanceresort.com

Sundance Catalog

At the base of the Sundance Village is a tiny store which guests would frequently write to, requesting special items they had seen while visiting Sundance. As a result, Robert Redford called together a few colleagues to discuss starting a mail-order catalog to fulfil these requests and make Sundance's unique items available to a wider audience. The first catalog was sent out in the fall of 1989. Now produced annually, the catalog has developed a loyal audience over the years. *www.sundancecatalog.com*

According to Robert Redford, the Sundance name itself comes from the Native American "sundance", a ritual associoted with the tribes that lived around Mt. Timpanogas. However, anyone with a passing interest in film will note that "Sundance" was also the name of the character Redford played in the 1969 seminal western, *Butch Cassidy and the Sundance Kid*.

The film was based on the escapades of real-life outlaws Butch Cassidy and Harry Longabaugh (who picked up his nickname whilst incarcerated in the Wyoming town). Ironically, Butch Cassidy did visit Park City during the late 1880s and hung around just long enough to rob one of the local saloons. However, there is no record of whether Longabaugh accompanied him on that particular outing.

the
city

"Park City itself? It's situated about 35 minutes from Salt Lake City and, during 10 days in January, several light years from anything resembling the real world."

John Anderson
Chief Film Critic, Newsday

"Obviously, I think Park City is the greatest place in the United States!"

Steven Soderbergh
Director

the city

Nestled high above modern-day Salt Lake City in the Wasatch Mountains, occupying 12 square miles of Utah's Summit County, lies the town of Park City, incorporated in 1884. Few of those who've actually been there would argue that Park City lives up to the size its name suggests. With a resident population of just over 7,500, it is little more than a town by most reckoning. But then, Park City has always been full of contradictions.

Beginning its life as little more than a stop on the road for weary travellers, Park City was blessed with two assets which shaped its future. During the late 19th century, the first phase of the town's prosperity was ushered in by the discovery of silver in the surrounding mountains. But as with nearly all precious metal "rushes" in America and abroad, prosperity proved fleeting. Within 70 years of the first strike, the mines were silent, the miners had departed, and the tumbleweed count seriously threatened to outnumber the human population by 10 to 1.

But instead of following the fate of other small mining towns, Park City was fortunate to be able to capitalise on its second asset: snow. The winter weather that had long been the bane of the prospectors' lives was an infinitely renewable resource, and over time, brought with it lasting prosperity that few former mining towns have enjoyed. Within a short 30 years of the last mine closing, Park City managed to transform itself into one of America's top winter destinations. The town now welcomes more than 17 million visitors a year and has one of the highest densities of non-resident home owners in the country (not to mention some staggering property prices). And just to ensure that Park City keeps everyone guessing, the city also plays host to one of the world's most prestigious film festivals.

park city facts

Population 7,500

Average Temperatures Winter 30°F (-1°C), Summer 80°F (27°C)

Average January Snowfall 31 inches (79 cm)

Time Zone U.S. Mountain Time (GMT -6)

Electricity 110 volts AC, 60Hz (standard North American flat two-pin plugs)

Phone Country Code 1, City Code 435

history

The area now occupied by Summit County was a traditional Indian hunting ground for many centuries before the first Europeans arrived in the region. Colonialism first touched the area in 1776, when Spanish Franciscan missionary-explorers Silvestre Velez de Escalante and Francisco Atanasio Domínguez stopped in the nearby Provo Valley during an expedition to discover a northern route between New Mexico and California. Almost 50 years later, the area was again visited by Europeans: In 1823, mountain explorer Jedediah Smith passed through the Kamas Valley on his way from Wyoming to California. Then in 1847, Brigham Young and the Mormon settlers came through on their way to the Salt Lake Valley. However, when it comes to Park City itself, the town has perhaps a slightly unflattering origin: It started its life as a tollbooth.

In the late 1840s, a local explorer by the name of Parley P. Pratt noticed the growing number of travellers moving through the area on their way to the California goldfields. Pratt had been charged by Brigham Young to lead an expedition to locate suitable areas in the mountains for new Mormon settlements and arranged the construction of a road from Salt Lake City to a site near present-day Park City. The road was opened in 1850, and the business of extracting tolls from fortune-hungry travellers necessitated the construction of a small settlement. This became known as Parley's Park because of the lush grasses and blazing wildflowers found there during the summer.

As the 1860s began, Brigham Young's Salt Lake City was booming, and in 1862, a troop of federal soldiers, under the leadership of Colonel Patrick Connor, was sent to Salt Lake to guard mail routes into the area. Although mail security was the primary mission, having a contingent of federal troops in the area also provided the Union generals with a convenient way of keeping an eye on the Mormons, whom some feared might side with the Confederacy during the Civil War. Almost from the first moment he arrived in Utah, Colonel Connor did not see eye to eye with Brigham Young, and ironically, this animosity proved to be the main catalyst for kick-starting Park City as a mining town.

Many of Connor's soldiers were in fact prospecting veterans of the California goldfields, and on seeing Parley's Park, immediately recognised the potential of the area for harbouring precious metal deposits. Connor figured that, much like what had happened following the discovery of gold in California, a significant metal strike in the Wasatch Mountains would result in a huge influx of outsiders. It was his hope that these outsiders would dilute the Mormon population, and with it, their power in the region. Consequently, he encouraged many of his soldiers to spend their leisure time prospecting in the mountains.

The soldiers located several small claims, but the first important mineral strikes came in 1868 and 1869, when rich veins of silver ore were discovered at the Emma and Flagstaff Mines in Little Cottonwood Canyon east of Salt Lake City. As Connor had foreseen, the discovery of precious metals generated a mining boom, and thousands of fortune-hungry prospectors descended on the area. Miners came from all over, including the California goldfields, the Nevada silver mines, and from as far away as Scotland, Ireland, and Scandinavia. Many of the immigrants were also Chinese, previously employed on the transcontinental railroad project and left to fend for themselves after its completion.

Between 1870 and 1900, the population of Parley's Park increased by around 40 percent, and the small settlement turned into a typical frontier town, with boarding houses, stores, saloons, schools, and, of course, brothels. In May 1872, prominent Salt Lake City politician George Snyder arrived with his family to settle in Parley's Park and, on seeing the bustling town, immediately dubbed it Parley's Park City. The nickname stuck, but was later shortened to Park City when the town was officially incorporated in 1884.

Meanwhile, mining operations in the area were booming. By the early 1880s, several dozen mines had popped up around the town, forming what came to be known as the Park City Mining District. These included the Crescent, the Anchor, the Mayflower, and the Ontario. Of the four major excavations, the Ontario Mine harboured an exceedingly rich vein of silver ore and, in its heyday, was considered to be one of the most valuable silver mines in the world. It was perhaps no surprise then, that the Ontario found its way into the hands of George Hearst, father of William Randolph Hearst, who purchased the mine shortly after its discovery in 1872

for what the owners considered a princely sum: $27,000. The mine went on to produce more than $50 million worth of silver before finally closing in the late 1950s.

But life in the new Park City wasn't all smooth sailing. In the prosperous days of the 1880s, the town went through a massive construction boom. Due to the necessity of speed, many of the new structures were built haphazardly, and most were made out of wood. This situation was a disaster waiting to happen. The warning signs went unheeded in 1882 and 1884, when two small, but relatively destructive, fires consumed a number of buildings in the town. Calamity struck on the morning of 29 June 1898, when a massive fire broke out in the commercial district. Dry canyon winds fanned the flames, and seven hours later, nearly three-quarters of the town had been destroyed. Once the dust settled, the Park City authorities had learnt their lesson, and a massive reconstruction project was commissioned, this time featuring brick and stone structures. However, it would take more than 20 years for Park City to recover from the destruction of the 1898 fire, still the worst in Utah history.

The turn of the 20th century saw Park City continue to grow on the back of its mineral wealth, although nothing like the boom days of the 1880s. Shortly after World War I, a month-long strike by the international workers in the mines forced the town's first significant slowdown. A series of further strikes during the 1920s also nibbled at the town's prosperity, but it was ultimately the Great Depression that tipped the scales. Continuing labour problems, a crash in the market for precious metals, and a steady decrease in the quality of the ore being excavated coalesced to push Park City into terminal decline. By 1950, fewer than 200 miners were working the remaining shafts, and Park City was in danger of becoming a ghost town.

Salvation arrived in 1963 in the form of a loan from the U.S. government's Area Redevelopment Agency. The money ($1.25 million) was combined with capital from private investors to build the Treasure Mountain Resort (now the Park City Mountain Resort) and ushered in the town's second boom. The winter conditions that had proved so troublesome for the miners breathed new life into Park City, transforming its economic base from mining to tourism. The quality and consistency of the snow in the area helped the town quickly establish itself as one of America's premiere winter sports destinations, and any lingering doubts about Park City's status as a world-class ski resort were dispelled when the town hosted nearly 40 percent of the events for the 2002 Winter Olympic Games.

Today, Park City is a year-round recreation destination, nestled 6,500–7,000 feet (2,015–2,170 metres) above sea level in the Wasatch Mountains. With more than 17 million visitors each year (97 percent of whom are American), tourism is Park City's main economic driver. Visitors enjoy not only the renowned winter sports facilities, but also a host of summer activities, including golf, horseback riding, fly-fishing, mountain-bike riding, and hunting. And, of course,

every January that small film festival rolls into town.

getting there

Park City is located in the Wasatch Mountains in the state of Utah, approximately 36 miles from Salt Lake City. Home to around 1.3 million people, Salt Lake City is served by a variety of transportation modes, so getting there poses few problems.

By Air
Salt Lake City International Airport (airport code: SLC, www.slcairport. com) is the main entry point for those flying to the festival. SLC International is one of the major airports in the western United States and is therefore well serviced by a variety of domestic and international carriers. Both Delta Airlines (www.delta.com) and Southwest Airlines (www.southwest. com) use the airport as a major hub, and at the time of writing, Delta (a festival sponsor) offered a special "meeting code" for discounted flights (see the Sundance Web site at www. sundance.org for more information). A number of the newer "low-cost" domestic carriers also fly to Salt Lake City; JetBlue Airways (www. jetblue.com) is one which is popular with penny-watching filmmakers, particularly the New York and L.A. crowds.

Whilst the options on flights to Salt Lake City should be reasonably plentiful, it's important to remember that January is the middle of the ski season in Utah. Consequently, you will not only be in competition with other festival attendees for seats, but also people who've booked ski holidays. To ensure that you not only get a seat, but also the best possible fare, it goes without saying that you should book your tickets as early as humanly possible. Today's airlines are masters of "dynamic pricing," which means the closer to the flying date you book your ticket, the more you will pay.

Approximate flight times to Salt Lake City from major US cities are as follows:

Atlanta	3:46
Boston	5:13
Chicago	3:18
Dallas	2:37
Houston	2:49
Kansas City	2:22
Los Angeles	1:48
Minneapolis	2:38
New York	5:26
Omaha	2:08
Orlando	4:31
Phoenix	1:24
San Francisco	1:46
Seattle	1:50
Washington, DC	4:31

These flight times are for direct flights to Salt Lake City from the particular city. Due to the huge number of domestic airlines and the hideously complex way in which U.S. air routes have been carved up, you may find that non-direct flights take considerably longer. It's always advisable to do your research and find out which airlines fly directly to Salt Lake City from your local airport (or entry airport, if you are flying in from overseas).

Once you've arrived at Salt Lake City, getting to Park City is pretty straightforward. Most people opt to use one of the various resort shuttle companies to take them the 36 miles to Park City. Shuttles leave the airport approximately every 15 to 20 minutes, and the journey time to Park City is around 45 minutes (however, this can be longer during Salt Lake City's morning and evening rush hours). Fares start at around $27 one way, but if you know your departure date, you can often save a few dollars by purchasing a round-trip ticket. Try Xpress Shuttle (Tel. Toll-Free 800-397-0773 or 801-596-1600, www. xpressshuttleutah.com), All Resort Express (Tel. Toll-Free 800-457-9457 or 435-649-3999, www.allresort.com) or Park City Shuttle (Tel. Toll-Free 888-658-2227 or 435-658-2227, www. parkcityshuttle.com). At the time of writing, the latter was offering to beat any competitor's rate by 10 percent. Although they aren't signposted very clearly, you can find the airport shuttle desks at the far end of the terminal on the same level as Baggage Claim.

A taxi from Salt Lake City International airport to Park City will probably set you back around $80 plus tip.

By Car
America was made for road trips, so if you have time on your hands, driving to Park City can be a load of fun. Most of the drivers tend to come from Southern California (with a requisite stopover in Las Vegas to warm up for the festival); however, a few adventurous souls have been known to hit the road from other parts of the country. If you plan on steering your car toward the open highway, expect the following drive times to Park City:

Los Angeles
11–12 hours
690 miles (1,110 km)

San Francisco
12–13 hours
766 miles (1,233 km)

New York
35–36 hours
2,152 miles (3,463 km)

Miami
42–43 hours
2,602 miles (4,187 km)

San Antonio
28–29 hours
1,417 miles (2,280 km)

Toronto
30–31 hours
1,882 miles (3,028 km)

Vancouver
16–17 hours
1,011 miles (1,627 km)

An alternative to driving the whole way is flying into Salt Lake City and picking up a rental car for the final leg to Park City. But before you start frantically hitting rental-company Web sites, consider whether a hired car is really worth the effort. If your festival accommodation and activities are all centred around Park City, getting a rental car is probably a waste of time. It will certainly be cheaper to get the airport shuttle to Park City, and the free city and festival buses will satisfy all your local transportation needs. You'll also be able to avoid the frustrations of severe restrictions on parking, loads of pedestrians getting in the

way, and huge traffic jams caused by everything from the mundane (a beer truck blocking Main Street in both directions while the driver unloads the amber neck massager one crate at a time), to the exciting (crowds that appear from nowhere to watch two A-list celebrities in a no-holds-barred slugfest over the last table at 350 Main...okay, that's a bit far-fetched, but you get the idea).

If you do decide to drive to Park City from Salt Lake, make sure you allow plenty of time. The Utah mountain weather in January can be erratic, and even the interstates are sometimes closed due to snow. To get to Park City, simply pick up Interstate 80 in Salt Lake City and follow it east for about 30 minutes. Take the exit for State Highway 224 at Kimball Junction and then follow that directly into Park City.

By Train
Amtrak trains service Salt Lake City from a huge number of cities around the US. For more information, visit www.amtrak.com. The main train station in Salt Lake City is located at 340 South 600 West, Salt Lake City, UT 84101. If you arrive in Salt Lake City by train, you will need to take a taxi to Park City.

By Coach
Greyhound coaches service Salt Lake City from many North American cities. The coach trip from L.A. takes about 14-16 hours, and from Vancouver, 25-29 hours. For more information, visit www.greyhound.com. As with the trains, if you arrive in Salt Lake City by coach, you will need to take a taxi to Park City.

finding your way

Most first-time visitors to the festival are surprised when they find out that Park City is, more accurately, just a reasonably small town. Although this creates some challenges in locating enough accommodation for festival events as well as festivalgoers, it also means that finding your way around is a breeze. Most of the action (for festival purposes, anyway) happens in a small number of places around town, and the only other things you are likely to need to find are your accommodation and perhaps a ski resort, if you are planning on hitting the slopes.

The town itself is loosely divided into nine main areas:

Historic District
The area around Main Street is the heart of the original town. A good many of the town's restaurants and bars are located in this area, and it is the main festival hub.

Prospector Square
This is one of the main districts of town outside the Historic District. This area contains a mix of residential and commercial buildings and a reasonable selection of hotels and eateries. Prospector Square is also another hub for the festival.

Park City Mountain Resort
The oldest ski resort in Park City is located on the western side of town near the Historic District. The area contains a mix of shops, hotels, and residential condos.

Park Meadows
A mainly private residential area north of Kearns Boulevard.

The Aerie
Another mainly residential area in the centre of town between Kearns Boulevard and Main Street.

Solamere
A mainly residential area on the eastern side of town behind the Aerie.

Ridge View
A mainly residential area at the northern end of town between Park Meadows and State Highway 224.

Deer Valley
One of the newest districts of Park City, Deer Valley is home to the Deer Valley Resort, another of the town's main ski areas. Deer Valley is also quite residential, and, outside of the resort, there are few shops or restaurants.

Silver Lake Village
High in the mountains to the south of town sits the swish Silver Lake Village. The village is home to hotels and restaurants which cater to the top end of the price scale.

The Canyons
Located just outside city limits, The Canyons is the newest of Park City's three main ski resorts. Although technically not part of Park City, The Canyons is useful for festivalgoers because it's a major source of accommodation and has a collection of local shops and restaurants. The Canyons is located off State Highway 224, northwest of town, and is far

enough from the Historic District to require a bus or car.

Once you arrive in Park City, one of your first missions should be to secure a good map of the town. You can pick up a free map from either branch of the Park City Chamber of Commerce's visitor-information centre:

Park City Visitor Information Center
750 Kearns Boulevard
Tel. 435-658-4541
www.parkcityinfo.com
Open 9am–6pm, 7 Days

Park City Historic Museum
528 Main Street
Tel. 435-649-6104
Open 10am–7pm, Mondays–Saturdays
12pm–6pm, Sundays

With map in hand and a basic understanding of the main districts of Park City, you should take a bit of time shortly after your arrival to familiarise yourself with the following places. Some of these house various functions of the festival; you will simply find it useful to know the locations of the others. Official festival information booths are also scattered around town and staffed with volunteers who can help you find your way. Here are the key festival venues at the present moment (keep in mind that they may change at any time):

Festival Headquarters (HQ)
The Park City Marriott Hotel at Prospector Square is transformed into Festival HQ for the duration of the event. (Note: There are two Marriott Hotels in Park City, Prospector Square and Summit Watch, so don't confuse them.) Here you will find the registration centre (register/pick up your credentials), the press office, sponsor and industry services, festival merchandise, the transportation and accommodation desks, and the various administrative arms of the festival. The Park City Marriott straddles a block between Prospector Avenue and Sidewinder Drive in the Prospector Square district.

Filmmaker Lodge
Local community venue the Elks Lodge gets a temporary name change during the festival, becoming the Filmmaker Lodge. Whilst the décor may be reminiscent of a style time forgot, the venue is a wonderful place to meet, network, or just hang out during the day. Filmmaker Lodge also provides café refreshments and plays host to a range of panel discussions and other events throughout the festival. You can find the Filmmaker Lodge at 550 Main Street (about a third of the way up on the left, if you are walking uphill). Festival credentials are required for entry.

Sundance Digital Center
The Sundance Film Festival Digital Center provides a centralised point for all of the festival's digital activities. Here you can explore the changing landscape of digital filmmaking, visit exhibits by a variety of equipment-manufacturer sponsors, attend forums on a range of issues relating to digital filmmaking, or simply sit back and enjoy a quiet coffee. The Digital Center also hosts the Sundance Online Film Festival, and provides free Internet access (both terminals and

wireless connections). The Sundance Digital Center is located downstairs in the Park City Mall at 333 Main Street (toward the top of the hill on the right).

Music Café

Local nightclub PLAN B takes on the duties of hosting the Sundance Film Festival Music Café. Throughout the Festival, a range of established and emerging artists perform during the day for your listening pleasure. Daytime performances are free to those with festival credentials. Evening performances are not officially part of the festival, and there may be a cover charge to attend. The Music Café is located on the left at the top of Main Street next to the Wasatch Brew Pub.

Sundance House

During the festival, the Kimball Art Center is transformed into Sundance House, playing host to a range of exhibits and events and providing several "studios" for use by visiting members of the press. Sundance House also offers free Internet access (both terminals and wireless connections) and has an excellent café for a quick meeting or a casual bite to eat. Sundance House is located on the corner of Park Avenue and Heber Avenue (just off the bottom of Main Street). Festival credentials are required for entry.

Main Festival Box Office

The main box office is the place to purchase tickets for screenings. Box-office hours are 10am– 7pm prior to the festival, and 8am–7pm during the event. The main box office is located in the Gateway Center at 136 Heber Avenue.

Festival Merchandise Store

You can pick up official festival merchandise from several stores around town. The "flagship" festival merchandise store is located in the Gateway Center with the festival box office and is open during the same hours. You can also purchase official Sundance gear at Festival HQ, the Eccles Theater, and online at www. sundance.org.

Cinemas

There are six main venues where films are screened in Park City during the festival. These are described in the *Screenings* section later in this guide.

In addition to the key festival venues, you'll also find it handy to know the location of the following city venues:

Main Street

Living up to its name, this is where the main festival action takes place. Cutting a line straight up the hill, Main Street is dotted with bars, restaurants, and galleries (selling locally produced items targeted mainly at the ski tourists). Main Street is also home to the Park City Post Office and a number of shops, including Dolly's Bookstore (at number 510) and a State Liquor Store.

Kearns Boulevard

This major road marks the northern boundary of the town for festival purposes. On Kearns Boulevard, you will find the Yarrow Hotel, Holiday Village Cinemas, and the Eccles Center, all of which are key festival screening venues.

Park Avenue

Park Avenue is the main route into town from Salt Lake City and is also a major thoroughfare between venues located along Kearns Boulevard and those around Main Street. With all of the punters heading into the Main Street area for the evening's revelry, gridlock is quite common on Park Avenue around sunset. Driving in this area is usually best avoided, and you may also find that it's quicker to walk between some venues than to take the shuttle. The Park City Library Center (another screening venue) is also found on Park Avenue.

Old Town Transit Center

Parallel to Main Street runs Swede Alley (named for the foreign miners who used to make their homes there), and on it you'll find the central bus station, known as the Old Town Transit Center. Almost all of the free city buses connect at this venue, and most festival shuttles also swing through (see *Getting Around* for more information).

Silver Mine

The old Ontario Silver Mine is now a museum with exhibits celebrating Park City's mining heritage and, during the festival, sometimes plays host to parties and other events. The Silver Mine is located high above Park City at the top of Bald Mountain. If there is a specific festival event being held, free shuttle buses run between the Old Town Transit Center and the Silver Mine.

Snow Park Lodge

A rather impressive wooden structure, the Snow Park Lodge provides a range of bars and shops for those staying in the Deer Valley area, but the venue is also for the site of parties during the festival. For specific events, free shuttle buses run between Snow Park Lodge and the Old Town Transit Center. At other times, city buses will take you there.

National Ability Center

Located about 15 minutes from Park City by car, the National Ability Center also hosts events and parties during the festival. For specific events, free shuttle buses run between the Old Town Transit Center and the National Ability Center.

Park City Racquet Club

For several years now, the Park City Racquet Club has hosted the festival's closing-night awards ceremony. You can find the Racquet Club at 1200 Little Kate Road in the Park Meadows area.

Sundance Village

Robert Redford's Sundance Village is located about an hour's drive from Park City in Provo Canyon at the foot of Mount Timpanogos. The Sundance Village is both a retreat and an arts centre and hosts a range of screenings and events during the festival. Complimentary shuttle buses run between Park City (Old Town Transit Center) and the Sundance Village for the duration of the event.

Festival and other relevant venues and locales are marked on the Park City map at the back of this book. You can also find a map of key festival venues in the Sundance film guide.

getting around

Although Park City was founded several decades before the invention of the automobile, you may wonder whether after the great fire, the town was reconstructed with wheels rather than legs in mind as the chief mode of transportation. Or perhaps it was simply the inclement winter weather that led town planners to discard the idea of walking as a means of getting about.

Whilst the areas of the old town around Main Street are relatively compact, the newer parts of Park City suffer from a mini-sprawl. Places can be extremely spread out, and in many cases, there are no sidewalks. This has produced an over reliance on cars for getting around, and indeed the number of SUVs per person in Park City must be one of the highest in the whole United States. At other times of the year, this probably doesn't pose too much of a problem; however, during the festival, it's another story entirely. Nothing jams the traffic on Main Street like a stretch SUV.

With the traffic, the distances, and the weather, getting around Park City during festival time can sometimes feel like a chore. Luckily for all concerned, transportation salvation comes in the form of the humble bus.

Festival Shuttle Buses
At a time lost in the annals of Sundance history, someone made a decision that a free bus service to ferry festivalgoers between venues would be a good idea. Whoever made that decision should be personally thanked by every one of the 40,000-odd festivalgoers who now make the trip to Park City. The free shuttle-bus system is one of the greatest things about attending the festival: Not only is the problem of getting around town through gridlock and bad weather solved, but this wonderfully egalitarian system presents a fantastic opportunity to socialise and make new friends.

The festival shuttle buses operate on a series of routes with predefined stops (look for the red signs). The service runs well into the wee hours, and the festival transportation office kindly adjusts the departure of the last shuttles to allow for any late-night screenings that run behind.

The following festival shuttle routes operate approximately every 10 minutes. Keep in mind that there are slight modifications in the schedules and routes every year, so it's best to check final running times either online or when you arrive in Park City. It's also worth noting that the shuttle services tends to finish earlier on the last day of the festival.

SFF Theatre Loop
A continuous service looping around the various festival screening venues. Stops: Festival HQ, Prospector Square Theatre, Eccles Theater, Yarrow and Holiday Theatres, Main Street (Old Town Transit Center), Library Center Theater, Yarrow and Holiday Theatres, Lot G (Eccles Theater Parking), Festival HQ.

Festival HQ/Eccles Loop
A short ride for those who object to walking the 400-odd yards between the two venues (or if the weather is bad). Stops: Festival HQ, Prospector Square Theater, Eccles Theater, Lot G (Eccles Theater Parking), Festival HQ.

Festival HQ/Main Street Loop-

The direct link between Main Street and Festival HQ at the Marriott Prospector Square, swinging by the key festival parking lots along the way. Stops: Festival HQ, Prospector Square Theater, Eccles Theater, Main Street (Old Town Transit Center), Lot G (Eccles Theater Parking), Festival HQ.

In addition to the regular shuttles, the festival also operates special services to and from specific event locations. Most of these buses travel between the Old Town Transit Center and the event venue, with service commencing a couple of hours before the start and continuing through to the end of the event. One thing to know about festival shuttles is that they only stop at designated festival stops and not city bus stops.

For the most up-to-date hours of operation and route information, visit the festival Web site (www.sundance. org) a month or so before the next festival.

City Buses

Park City Transit runs an extensive bus network throughout the town and surrounding areas, and by some minor miracle in today's world, this service is also completely free. Whilst the festival shuttles are generally better because of fewer stops, city buses provide an excellent alternative if you are not near a festival shuttle stop, a festival bus is full, or you want to travel between your accommodation and festival venues.

City buses run every 10 to 20 minutes from 6:30am to 2:30am daily (the last bus is at 2am) and can be picked up at any city bus stop — look for the blue signs. The following routes are in operation:

Bus 1 (Orange)

Main Street — Deer Valley

Bus 2 (Red)

Main Street — Park City Mountain Resort — Prospector Square

Bus 3 (Dark Green)

Main Street — Park City Mountain Resort — Park Meadows

Bus 4 (Blue)

Main Street — Deer Valley — Silver Lake Village

Bus 5 (Purple)

Main Street — Park City Mountain Resort — Thaynes Canyon

Bus 6 (Yellow)

Main Street — Prospector Square Express

Bus 7 (Light Green)

Main Street — Park City Mountain Resort — Prospector Square — The Canyons

Bus 8 (Brown)

Main Street — Park City Mountain Resort — The Canyons — Kimball Junction

Main Street Trolley

Travels up and down Main Street

Unlike festival buses, city buses stop at both festival and city bus stops. You can obtain a complete timetable and route map for the city bus service from http://www.parkcity. org/visiting/getting_around/maps. html (PDF) and more information from the Park City Transit Web site (www. parkcity.org; look under "Residents, Transportation" on the main menu).

Walking

After the shuttle buses, walking is probably the next quickest way of getting between festival venues (so long as there isn't a major blizzard). The longest walk is between Main Street and Festival HQ, but at about 20 to 30 minutes, even it is doable (although take care at the Prospector Square end of the walk, as the traffic on Deer Valley Drive often moves like there's no tomorrow). Some routes (such as Festival HQ to the Eccles Theater or the Library Center Theater to Main Street) can be walked in less time than it takes to wait for the shuttle. A word of caution, however, for those considering a stroll in Park City during the festival: Watch out for ice!

Taxis

Using taxis to get around festival venues in Park City is largely unnecessary; however, if you're staying out of town, you may find them useful to get between your accommodation and festival venues. It is sometimes possible to hail taxis on Main Street; however, in all likelihood, you will need to order one over the phone. Several cab companies operate in Park City, and you should expect to pay the same sort of rates as you do in any major town:

ACE Cab Company
Tel. 435-649-8294

Citiride Taxi Service
Tel. 435-658-2220

Music Taxi
Tel. 435-649-6496

Powder for the People
Tel. 435-649-6648

Park City Cabs
Tel. 435-658-2227

Driving (and Parking)

With the extensive festival and city bus system, driving in Park City is an aggravation you can largely avoid. Two main obstacles face those who plan to use a car as their primary mode of transportation around town during the festival: traffic and parking (although inclement weather can also add insult to injury).

The slightly less frustrating of the two is definitely traffic; however, it is still a good enough reason to avoid driving in town during the festival. The problem is particularly acute in the late afternoon/early evening (although if you're from L.A., you'll probably feel right at home). As dusk approaches, it is common to find gridlock on Main Street and Park Avenue, a situation exacerbated by road closures and crowds of festivalgoers starting out on the evening's revelry. Even at other times, traffic can be heavy, particularly on and around Main Street during the day as delivery trucks block access as they go about their business.

The other problem, parking, is far more frustrating. The Historic District of Park City around Main Street (where the bulk of the festival action is concentrated) doesn't enjoy the same abundance of open space as newer parts of town. Parking in this area is extremely limited, heavily restricted, and, of course, actively policed. And although there are quite a few parking lots in Park City, most are officially designated off limits to festivalgoers, with No Festival Parking signs a common sight around town.

So the advice is, if you're staying in Park City itself, leave the car at your accommodation and use the festival and city buses. If you're staying away from the centre of town, or in one of the neighbouring areas, your best bet is to use your car to get as close to a city or festival bus stop as possible, then park and ride.

If you get into town early in the day, you may be able to take advantage of the three official festival parking lots; however, spaces fill up quickly, and illegally parked cars will be towed. Two of the lots are located in the Prospector Square area: one on Prospector Avenue not far from the Prospector Square Theater (known as Lot G), and the other one adjacent to Festival HQ on Prospector Avenue (known as Lot F). The third lot is opposite the Library Center Theatre on Park Avenue. Daytime and evening parking is free; however, overnight parking is prohibited. Be sure and watch for reserved or permit-only places because not all the spaces in these three lots are available for festival parking. Lot G and the Library Center Theater lot are serviced by festival buses, and all three lots have city bus stops.

Paid parking is also available at several lots across town, although prices and maximum stays vary quite a bit. Limited "pay and display" parking is available on Main Street and in Swede Alley; however, the maximum stay for most spots is about four hours. There is also a paid underground parking lot on lower Main Street at the Marriott Summit Watch, and a covered pay lot near the Old Town Transit Center in Swede Alley. If you have a serious need to use your car in Park City, several temporary valet services are operated by enterprising locals in the downtown area (although obviously you will pay handsomely for the privilege).

Alternatively, in the past a limited number of Eccles Theater parking passes have been available from the Park City High School. To secure one, you'll need to lay around $250 on the table, but the money goes to a good cause — the Park City High School Fine Arts Department. For more information on Eccles Theater parking passes, visit the festival Web site (www.sundance.org).

parking wisdom...

In the past, the Festival has provided a series of handy parking hints entitled *Places Not to Park In Park City (Or How to Avoid Getting Fined or Towed)*. Heed the advice and don't park in these places during the day (parking is permitted at some of them late in the afternoon or in the evening): Park City Mountain Resort (outdoor lots), Park City High School, McPolin Elementary School, Treasure Mountain Middle School, Holiday Village Cinemas, Snow Creek Parking, the lot adjacent to Albertsons supermarket, or anywhere that you see the red No Festival Parking signs.

Many special events, such as the official parties, are held outside the downtown area of Park City, so even if you've been using buses to get around during the day, you may be tempted by the convenience of a car to get back from an event later on. Again, this is strongly discouraged as most venues hosting special events during the festival have little or no parking available. Thankfully, special festival shuttle buses service all official events, so you can continue to park and ride.

Finally, most Sundance veterans advise paying careful attention to the parking signs, particularly the red curbs (no parking), which can easily be obscured by even a minor snowfall. If you do run afoul of the parking authorities and find your car has mysteriously disappeared, there's a good chance it's been towed. You will need to contact either Park City Towing (Tel. 435-645-7775) or Park City Police Dispatch (Tel. 435-615-5500) and warm up your checkbook or credit card to secure the car's release.

accommodation

As in virtually every town or city that hosts a major event for visitors, finding well-located and reasonably priced accommodation is the biggest challenge facing most festival attendees. In Park City's case, the main problem is that the vast majority of accommodation service providers assume that you're coming to Park City to ski, and therefore you must be rich. If you're travelling on an expense account, this probably isn't an issue, but for many Sundancers, that's not the case. Reasonably priced accommodation options in Park City are limited and fill up very quickly. It therefore goes without saying that you should book your accommodation as far ahead as humanly possible and use every connection, excuse, and contact at your disposal to do so.

As far as official services go, the Park City Visitor Information Center (both branches) can provide lists of various options in the town and the surrounding areas. However, unlike many other municipal tourist offices, the personnel will not make arrangements on your behalf (although they will let you use their phone to make calls if you arrive in Park City without pre-booked accommodation). The Visitor Center also provides an online lodging locator in the Travel section of the official tourism Web site at www.parkcityinfo.com.

Budget Options

Budget accommodation options are few and far between in Park City, but they aren't entirely nonexistent. A couple of choices are available if you book early enough.

Chateau Aprés Lodge

Probably the best budget option in Park City, Chateau Aprés is conveniently located just off Park Avenue and has private rooms for one to four people, plus male and female dorms. Continental breakfast is included in the price, and all rooms (except dorms) have private bathrooms, cable TV, telephones, and daily maid service.

Prices start at around $85 per night for one-to-two person rooms and go up to about $105 per night for a four-person room. Dorm places are approximately $30 per night.

Chateau Aprés Lodge
1299 Norfolk Avenue
P.O. Box 579
Park City, Utah 84060
Tel. 435-649-9372
Toll-Free 800-357-3556
Fax. 435-649-5963
www.chateauapres.com

Park City Base Camp

Previously known as the Park City International Hostel, PC Base Camp is conveniently located on Main Street. It has 16 mini-dorm rooms, each with four beds in two-bunk configuration. There are no curfews or lockouts, and the facilities include a kitchen, lounge, laundry, TV room, and free Internet access. Bunks in Park City Base Camp are around $50 per night during the film festival (up from around $35 per night at other times during the winter). Prices are exclusive of tax, which adds around 10 percent to the total. Bookings usually open in mid-December each year.

Park City Base Camp
268 Main Street
Park City, UT 84098
Tel. Toll-Free 888-980-7244
www.parkcitybasecamp.com

Hotels

Since tourism is the main business in Park City, the hotel density is considerably higher than in a town of similar size elsewhere. If money is not really an object, arranging accommodation for the festival

should pose little problem (assuming you book early enough, of course).

Park City has a range of hotels to cater to most budgets, from two-star motels through five-star resorts. A night in a hotel starts around $75 and goes higher than most of us like to contemplate. Most rooms, however, are generally in the $100 to $300 per night range. Try the following hotels:

Park City Marriott

1895 Sidewinder Drive
P.O. Box 4439
Park City, UT 84060
Tel. 435-649-2900
Toll-Free 800-234-9003
www.marriotthotels.com/slcpc

Prospector Square Lodge

2200 Sidewinder Drive
Park City, UT 84098
Tel. 435-649-7100
Toll-Free 800-453-3812
www.prospectorlodging.com

Silver King Hotel

1485 Empire Avenue
Park City, UT 84060
Tel. 435-649-5500
Toll-Free 800-331-8652
www.silverkinghotel.com

The Yarrow Resort Hotel

1800 Park Avenue
Park City, UT 84060
Tel. 435-649-7000
Toll-Free 800-927-7694
www.yarrowresort.com

B&Bs

Private bed and breakfasts are reasonably abundant in Park City and the surrounding areas. Rates start at around $90 per night and go up. B&Bs are a good option if hotel accommodation is hard to find, although hotels are generally preferable. Since many B&Bs are also the owners' private homes, they can sometimes have more restrictive regimes than hotels in a similar price range. This can mean curfews and stricter rules about what you can and can't do in your room.

Condos

One of the most popular accommodation options in Park City with both festivalgoers and skiers is renting a condo. Local (and not so local) entrepreneurs have been quick to capitalise on the demand for self-contained accommodation for almost every size group and price range. Condo complexes are abundant throughout Park City and come in a range of shapes and sizes from studios up to residences suitable for 8 to 10 people. Prices during the festival start at around $180 per night and max out around $500. Most condo rentals are managed by third-party agencies, which is good because it makes it easier to search a range of options at one time, but bad because it entails commissions (paid by the landlord), which ultimately push the prices up. However, if you're travelling to Sundance with a group, renting a condo will most likely be the cheapest option available. Try the following lodging agencies for starters:

Central Reservations of Park City
Tel. 435-649-6606
Toll-Free 800-570-1276
www.resortquestparkcity.com/sff

David Holland's Resort Lodging
Tel. 435-655-3315
Toll-Free 888-PARKCITY
www.davidhollands.com

Deer Valley Lodging
Tel. 435-649-4040
Toll-Free 800-453-3833
www.deervalleylodging.com

Identity Properties
Tel. 435-649-5100
Toll-Free 800-245-6417
www.pclodge.com

Private Homes

A high proportion of the houses in Park City are actually second homes, owned by wealthy people who spend a good deal of their time living elsewhere. Consequently, during the festival, many homes are available for rental, so if you have a large group or simply want to wallow in the lap of luxury, these can be a great option. Most private-home rentals are managed by the same people who look after condo rentals.

Staying Outside of Park City

If you're booking late and find it hard to locate something suitable in Park City (and you have a car), staying in one of the surrounding areas is an excellent alternative to building an igloo on the high-school football field (which may be your only other budget option). Keetley Junction, Kimball Junction, Silver Springs, Snyderville, Atkinson, and Gorgosa are doable options; likewise, Summit Park or Cranmer is also worth a shot. For a more typical Utah experience, you can also consider staying in Heber City (about 25 minutes away by car).

It is even possible to stay in Salt Lake City, but the commute back after a late-night event (particularly if the weather is bad) makes it a lot more hassle than it's really worth; and there's also a risk that you will feel isolated from the festival action. In saying that, every film in the festival does screen at least once in Salt Lake City, so if you're just hitting Sundance for the movies and want to avoid the crowds, staying in Salt Lake may not be such a bad option afterall.

An extensive list of hotels, B&Bs, and condo booking services can be found in Appendix V.

eating

Since it is one of Utah's top visitor destinations, it comes as no surprise that eateries of all types abound in Park City. Indeed, the town boasts that there are more chefs in Park City per capita than in Paris. Whether this is true or not, you certainly won't be hard up for choices when it's time for a feed, regardless of the type of cuisine you desire, or, to a large extent, the price you want to pay.

Most of the restaurants in Park City are concentrated in the Historic District, on and around Main Street. There are options here to suit most budgets. However, since the majority of people gravitate to this area once the evening sets in, competition for tables at many of these restaurants can be extremely fierce. One thing that some festivalgoers tend to forget is that there is more to dining

in Park City than Main Street: Plenty of decent eateries are located in other parts of the town, too. Several good options exist in the Prospector Square area, and the large resorts such as Deer Valley, Silver Lake, and The Canyons also provide a range of options for their guests and outside visitors.

Regardless of where you choose to eat, if you want to guarantee a table at most restaurants in Park City (or even just have control over when you eat), it's advisable to make reservations. With restaurant seats at a premium, many places are booked in advance by Hollywood types with per diem to burn. For some of the flashier restaurants on Main Street, such as Grappa, Chimayo, 350 Main, and Robert Redford's Zoom, dinner reservations need to be made several days ahead, if not before the festival. At other places, you can often get away without reservations, although inevitably there will be a wait during peak times.

Basic Options
For those on a tight budget, several inexpensive options are available. As with virtually every American town, corporate fast food is present to serve you the same stuff you're used to eating the world over. At the corner of Park Avenue and Iron Horse Drive, you'll find Burger King, Starbucks, and

parking city dining

The *Sundance — A Festival Virgin's Guide* Web site includes a large database of eateries across the full spectrum of styles and prices. The database also includes reviews, contact details, and a "restaurant basket" to help you plan your Park City eating experience. *www.sundanceguide.net*

Quizno's Classic Subs (a Subway-a-like with a toaster). Subway itself is located at the corner of Kearns Boulevard and Bonanza Drive, next to the utterly awful Taco Maker. There's a Pizza Hut (Tel. 435-649-3838) on Sidewinder Drive and a Domino's Pizza (Tel. 435-649-7788) on Kearns Boulevard. If you're desperate for it, McDonald's, Taco Bell, and Arby's can all be found on North Landmark Drive at Kimball Junction, but you'll need a car to get to them.

Slightly more upscale, but still a great value for the money, is the Windy Ridge Café at 1250 Iron Horse Drive, or the Off Main Café at 1782 Prospector Avenue for sandwiches, salads, and other typical café fare. El Chubasco in the Park City Plaza on Bonanza Drive (near the intersection with Kearns Boulevard) has traditional and inexpensive Mexican food; across the parking lot, you'll find Mountain Chicken, which does rotisserie chicken and ribs and boasts that its free-range birds never feel the chill of a freezer.

With a variety of options, including omelettes, sandwiches, and burgers, the Main Street Deli — you guessed it, on Main Street — is a popular choice for breakfast or lunch amongst those keeping an eye on their pennies. The financially challenged have also been known to gravitate to the excellent-value home cooking at the Corner Café inside the Yarrow Hotel (corner of Park Avenue and Kearns Boulevard).

The other tried and tested method for keeping hunger at bay is, of course, party food. Most parties include at least some finger food, so as long as you get invited, you shouldn't starve. Most of the official parties also include some form of buffet, although you need to get there early to avoid missing out.

Middle of the Road

The vast majority of eating options in Park City fit into this category, so it tends to be more about personal preference than anything else. For starters, try Burgies on Main Street for burgers, grills, and melts in a bar atmosphere; the Wasatch Brew Pub, also on Main Street, which does sandwiches, pizza, burgers, and has a host of locally brewed beers to sample; Lakota, the excellent café/brasserie in the Caledonian Hotel (corner of 7th Avenue and Main), which does a range of American and Continental dishes in a fairly laid-back environment; or La Casita at the bottom of Main Street, which most of the locals agree has the best Mexican food in Park City.

Other middle of the road suggestions include these:

Blind Dog Grill
(Salads/Grills/Seafood)
1781 Sidewinder Drive

The Claimjumper
(Pub/Steak House)
573 Main Street

Davanza's Pizzeria
(Pizza/Pasta/Burgers)
690 Park Avenue

The Eating Establishment
(Breakfast/Salads/BBQ/Pasta)
317 Main Street

Main Street Pizza & Noodle
(Sandwiches/Pizza/Pasta)
530 Main Street

Red Banjo Pizza
(Pizza/Pasta)
322 Main Street

Wok on Main
(Chinese)
438 Main Street

Top of the Line

For those with expense accounts or gold cards, Park City dining can be enjoyed at its finest. Robert Redford's Zoom at the corner of Main Street and Heber Avenue is always jammed during the festival (and, in reality, does cater to a range of budgets), and the "New American Brasserie," 350 Main, is popular with the chic crowd. Those fond of upscale Tex-Mex tend to gravitate to Chimayo (368 Main Street), while lovers of fine Italian food can be found at Grappa (151 Main Street) or Cicero's (306 Main Street).

For an alternative dining experience, a trip to the Tree Room at the Sundance Village for "earth to table" cuisine is a wonderful night out, although driving puts serious limitations on your ability to sample the excellent wine list. "Intimate Nouvelle French" dining is offered at Chenéz (Marriott Summit Watch Plaza, Lower Main Street), and the swish Silver Lake Village is home to a range of top-end fusion eateries, including the Goldener Hirsch Inn (7570 Royal Street East), the Mariposa (7620 Royal Street East), and Sai-Sommet (7720 Royal Street East).

Self-Catering

When it comes to eating, many Sundancers staying in condos opt for self-catering, particularly if they're travelling light in the wallet department. The needs of self-caterers are met at Albertsons supermarket on Park Avenue next to the Yarrow Hotel. Albertsons is open 24 hours and has a large pharmacy (although the pharmacy hours are 9am–9pm, and it closes earlier on weekends). For convenience items and quick snacks, there are two 7-Eleven stores in Park City: One is located on Park Avenue about halfway between Main Street and the Library Center; the other can be found at the corner of Sidewinder Drive and Kearns Boulevard.

money

Money matters in Park City during the festival are, on the whole, pretty straightforward. If you're planning on doing the festival cheaply, you can probably get by on $20 to $30 per day, after you've paid for your transportation to Park City, accommodation, and festival pass/package. You may even be able to do it cheaper if you are sharing lodging and can eat in. If you're planning to live it up a little, it is realistic to allow more like $50 to $100 per day (assuming you aren't eating in very fancy restaurants all the time).

Alternatively, you can just behave like a pro, slap everything on your credit card, have a great time, and worry about it later! Major credit cards (Visa/MasterCard/American Express/Discover) are accepted by nearly all establishments across town, and it certainly doesn't feel as bad when you pop an expensive restaurant bill on plastic as it does when you hand over a wad of cash.

If you are planning to travel with a non-major credit card, it's best to contact your card issuer before you leave home to confirm that it will be accepted in Park City. This is especially important for international visitors.

Banks and ATMs
If you take away all of the visitors, the population of Park City is relatively small; consequently, there aren't that many banks in town. Big American banking is represented by Bank One, with a branch on Park Avenue (with ATM), and Wells Fargo, which maintains a reasonable-sized branch with a drive-through ATM on the corner of Kearns Boulevard and Monitor Drive. The local Utah Zions Bank is also present in Park City, with the main branch on Kearns Boulevard near the junction with Park Avenue, and a small satellite branch up the Main Street end of Park Avenue. Both branches have ATMs.

Non-affiliated ATMs are in plentiful supply across town and can be found in many places including shops, bars, and restaurants. However, expect to pay a surcharge of $1 to $2 when you make a withdrawal from most of these machines. Indeed, virtually every ATM in Park City levies surcharges on withdrawals unless you are a customer of the bank which operates the machine. The one notable exception to this charging policy is Wells Fargo, which, at the time of writing, did not charge for ATM withdrawals.

Most ATMs also accept major credit cards and some international debit cards (such as Switch, Cirrus, and Maestro), but again, always confirm with the issuer that your card will be accepted before leaving home. It's also worth finding out the fees connected with cash withdrawals using your card as these can sometimes be quite high (particularly with Cirrus and Maestro).

Sales Tax
State and local sales taxes (similar to European VAT or Australian/Canadian GST) are levied on most purchases in the United States. The level of taxation varies from state to state, often even from county to county. In Park City, the sales taxes work out to be approximately 6.45 percent on top of the purchase price. International visitors who are used to taxes being included in prices should remember that virtually all figures displayed on merchandise in the U.S.A. do not include sales tax. Taxes will be added when you complete your purchase at the counter, so don't be surprised when the final price is a little higher than the tag indicates.

Currency Conversion
Currency conversion is of course not an issue if you're travelling to Park City from another part of the U.S.; however, for international visitors, a few greenbacks are necessary to see you through the festival. Exchange rates vary all the time, so always check the current rates before you travel. It's also a good idea to exchange all of your currency either before you leave home or at the Salt Lake City airport. Exchange facilities in Park City are virtually nonexistent,

and the one or two places that change money make you pay dearly for the privilege.

As a rough guide, you can expect the following exchange rates for major currencies:

Australian Dollars
1 AUD = 0.7 USD
1 USD = 1.4 AUD

British Pounds
1 GBP = 1.8 USD
1 USD = 0.5 GBP
Canadian Dollars
1 CAD = 0.7 USD
1 USD = 1.3 CAD

Euros
1 EUR = 1.2 USD
1 USD = 0.8 EUR

New Zealand Dollars
1 NZD = 0.6 USD
1 USD = 1.5 NZD

South African Rand
1 ZAR = 0.2 USD
1 USD = 6 ZAR

Visit OANDA (www.oanda.com) for up-to-the-second currency exchange rates and print out a miniature "cheat sheet" to take with you to Park City.

Tipping
In the U.S., it's customary to tip waiters and taxi drivers between 15 and 20 percent, more for unusually good service, less for bad service. Porters at airports and hotels expect $1 per bag, and if you're staying in a hotel, your maid will also expect a tip to ensure that your room stays clean for the duration of your visit.

International visitors should also be aware that you need to tip bar staff 15 to 20 percent when you buy a drink. If you are running a tab or paying by credit card, tip when you settle up. Otherwise, it's a good idea to "front load" your tip with the first order to ensure you receive speedy service on the next trip to the bar.

general information

New towns (and countries) can often throw a few curveballs to visitors. Here is a collection of handy hints and tips about Park City, and Utah in general, to help make your stay as smooth as possible.

Altitude
Most of Park City is between 6,500 and 7,000 feet (1,980–2,130 meters) above sea level, and some of the mountain recreation areas are as high as 10,000 feet (3,050 meters). At these altitudes, the air is a little thinner than many people are used to, and this, combined with the fact that the air is also extremely dry, can result in rapid dehydration. You can combat this by drinking plenty of water and pacing yourself to compensate for the fact that the effects of exercise (and alcohol) are exaggerated by the altitude.

Weather
With an average January snowfall of almost 31 inches (79 cm) Park City is alpine in every sense of the word. During the day, the temperature gets up to around 33°F (1°C). If the sun is out and you're walking around, it feels quite warm. However, even on a clear day, the sun can feel

deceptively weak, so remember to pack a good sunscreen. After dark, the temperature drops rapidly and can be as low as 12°F (-11°C) by the time you leave a late screening or evening party. Be sure and dress accordingly.

What to Wear

Given the attitude and time of year, it goes without saying that the keyword for Sundance attire is *warm*. Gloves, beanies (don't worry, there will always be someone who looks sillier than you in one of them), and warm jackets are a must for any more than a few minutes outside. Actually, a better word is probably *layers* since, after a bit of walking around, you can start to feel a little toasty, but the deep freeze returns quickly if you're not in the sun. Also pack a solid, comfortable pair of walking boots since you will be doing a lot of pavement pounding, and the snow and ice can be treacherous.

Keeping that in mind...ladies, it's probably best to resist the temptation to wear glamorous shoes for an evening out, unless you're lucky enough to have a (literally) door-to-door taxi service. Aside from the hazards of ice and the fact you may lose your toes to frostbite at any moment, one step in brown slushy water will see you consigning your expensive footwear to Park City's strangest landmark: the Shoe Tree (a kind of arboretum for deceased footwear next to the Marriott Summit Watch).

Smoking

With the Mormon aversion to drugs of all kinds, and the increasing amount of litigation involving second-hand smoke, Utah has taken a leaf out of the California book when it comes to public policy on smoking. Lighting up is prohibited in most official buildings and is generally controlled (if not banned outright) in many other places such as restaurants and bars. Establishments that allow smoking are usually sign-posted appropriately, but in many other places, smoking may only be allowed in designated areas. It's therefore always best to check before lighting up.

Internet Access

Checking email is now an essential daily task for most of us, and thankfully, getting online while you're in Park City is entirely straightforward. During the festival, free Internet terminals are available at several official venues, including Sundance House, the Digital Center, and Festival HQ. Sundance House and the Digital Center also offer free wireless hotspots for those travelling with a wi-fi-enabled laptop or other device. Outside of the official venues, many hotels offer Internet access for their guests, and you can also get 30 minutes online for free at the Park City Library Center. If you're planning on using the library services, put your name on the list at the reception desk and wait for a free terminal. Getting there early in the day is also a must as lines become a problem as the day drags on.

If you have exhausted all of the free Internet options and are desperate to get online, there are a couple of Internet Cafés in Park City where you can pay for access. These are listed in Appendix II.

Liquor Laws

It's more than likely that the reputation of Utah's "unusual" liquor laws preceded your visit. The joke goes that the laws were relaxed for the 2002 Olympics, basically making them "almost normal." In reality, things are not as bad as they are made out to be, particularly in a resort town like Park City.

There are four types of liquor licenses that venues in Utah can have:

Off-Sale License
Supermarkets and convenience stores are allowed to sell beer with an alcohol content of 3.2 percent or less by volume (in other words, light beer.) State-owned liquor stores can sell packaged alcohol of all types.

Tavern License
Patrons can be served light beer (again, 3.2 percent or less) for consumption on the premises without a meal.

Private-Club License
Those who become members of the club may be served alcohol of any type for consumption on the premises without purchasing a meal.

Restaurant License
Patrons who are having a meal can purchase alcohol of any type for consumption on the premises (although the types of alcohol available are at the discretion of the restaurant's management).

So far as eating in a restaurant or purchasing take-away alcohol goes, the laws are much the same as everywhere else. The main differences are that liquor stores are all state owned, and prices are slightly higher than you may be used to as a result of extra state taxes on alcohol. However, foreigners will probably still find prices cheaper than at home. A list of liquor stores in Park City can be found in Appendix II. You should note that all liquor stores are closed on Sundays and public holidays.

Most bars, pubs, and nightclubs operate under private-club licenses. As a result, you often see them advertised as "a private club for members only." Don't worry... this doesn't mean you can't get in. Advertising venues as private clubs is simply a way of maintaining the status quo with the state's ultraconservative legislators. For a nominal membership fee (aka cover charge), you, too, can join the esteemed membership ranks of most Park City private clubs. Alternatively, you can simply get an existing member to "sponsor" you as a guest for your visit to satisfy all the legal requirements. Locating a sponsor is a great way of meeting new people in a bar, and the generally accepted repayment for such kindness is to buy the sponsoring member a drink!

Finally, as with pretty much every other state in America, the legal drinking age is 21. International visitors should be prepared to be asked for ID more often than they are at home, and the type of ID accepted varies from venue to venue. Your passport is always the best bet if you think there's any chance that you can be taken for someone under 21.

Public Holidays
There isn't a huge impact on the

festival from public holidays, except that government buildings, banks, and, of course, the State Liquor Stores are all closed. There's only one public holiday that sometimes falls during the festival: Martin Luther King's Birthday, usually on the third Monday in January.

Personal Security

The small-town atmosphere of Park City makes it an extremely safe place with regard to personal security, particularly for those whose common sense prevails. The types of petty crime (such as pickpocketing) found at similar festivals in other cities are refreshingly absent, and incidents of violent crime are extremely rare. As always, women should take the usual precautions when travelling alone at night, and, as in most parts of the U.S., hitchhiking is not recommended.

Lost and Found

It goes without saying that you should always be vigilant with your personal belongings and ensure you take everything with you when you leave a place where you've been for more than a couple of minutes. If you are unfortunate enough to lose something, your first point of contact should be the venue where you think you may have left it. All lost property is stored at the venue where it is found for the duration of the festival, then transferred to the Sundance Institute offices in Salt Lake City (Tel. 801-328-3456) at the end of the event. Items not claimed from the Institute within two weeks of the festival closing are donated to charity. If you think you may have left something on a bus, the Park City Transit Lost Property Office is open from 8am to 5pm, Monday to Friday, and can be reached at 435-615-5301.

Telephones

Most pay phones in Park City take coins; however, you'll be much better off using a prepaid phone card. Pick these up from convenience stores such as 7-Eleven or Albertsons. Foreigners should be aware that you need to dial 1 before most phone numbers from public phones. The area code for Park City is 435, so calls to most other numbers (except 800 numbers, which are free) are considered long distance and are therefore more expensive. Calls to mobile (aka cell) phones are also charged at a higher rate (detailed information on using mobile phones can be found in Appendix IV). To make an international call, dial 011 (unless directed differently by the phone company), followed by the

welcome PIBs

The explosion of interest in the Sundance Film Festival during the 1990s brought a slight sense of amusement to Park City locals. For 10 days a year, the audacious colours of most fashionable skiwear are replaced by the uniform shade of the successful (but not always) film-industry executive: black. At some point along the way, somebody coined the phrase "people in black", or PIBs for short, to describe the "too hip for this town" (read, "inappropriately dressed for the weather") denizens in dark clothing, who seem to prowl Main Street continuously during the festival with mobile phones surgically attached to their ears.

code for the country you are calling, the area code (minus any leading 0), and finally, the local number.

Electricity
The electricity supply in North America is different to that found in Europe, Australia/New Zealand, and much of Asia. You need to ensure that any electrical devices you bring to the festival are multiregional; if not, you need to use a transformer. North American power operates with 115 volts at 60 hertz, whereas Europe/ Australia/Asia are on 220–240 volts at 50 hertz. Fortunately, because the voltages in North America are lower, there is less risk of blowing up your appliance than Americans face when they travel; however, it still isn't worth the risk. Also to make your device compatible, you need an appropriate adaptor to convert your plug to the double-flat-pin model used in North America.

Time Difference
Park City operates on U.S. Mountain Time, which is six hours behind Greenwich Mean Time (GMT). This translates to one hour ahead of U.S. Pacific Time, one hour behind U.S. Central Time, and two hours behind U.S. Eastern Time. Park City is six hours behind the U.K., and seven hours behind the rest of Western Europe. Southern Hemisphere visitors should also remember to take into account local summer time (aka daylight savings) when determining Park City time. If you prefer to let someone else worry about all this "one hour forward, two hours back stuff," try the World Time Server at www.worldtimeserver. com.

getting away

Attending any film festival can be an amazing experience, but it can also be very draining. Late nights (usually involving too much alcohol), early starts, and far too many screenings have the power to take it out of even the most seasoned campaigner. And this effect increases exponentially if you're attending a festival with a business agenda. Fortunately, many festivals take place in locations where there are a range of interesting ways to take time out and recharge. Sundance is no exception.

Outside of the festival, Park City is one of the most popular recreational destinations in America. Each year over 17 million visitors arrive in the town, of which only 40,000 are actually attending Sundance. The vast majority of people spend their time involved in a whole host of activities that have nothing to do with film. So if and when you need a break, the range of alternatives should never leave you at a loss for choices.

Winter Sports
The Park City of today owes its status and prosperity to one thing alone: exceptional snow. Since winter sports are the number-one reason most people come to the town, a variety of activities are available for all skill levels. If you're planning on being in Park City for the entire festival, it would be a shame not to test out what is reputedly some of the best snow on the planet. After all, they didn't hold over one-third of the 2002 Winter Olympic events in Park City for nothing. The mountains are also comparatively empty during Sundance since holiday skiers tend

to steer clear of the town at festival time.

Park City has three main ski resorts:

Deer Valley Resort
P.O. Box 1525
Park City, UT 84060
Tel. 435-649-1000
Toll-Free 800-424-DEER
Fax. 435-645-6939
www.deervalley.com

Park City Mountain Resort
1310 Lowell Avenue
P.O. Box 39
Park City, UT 84060
Tel. 435-649-8111
Toll-Free 800-222-PARK
Fax. 435-647-5374
www.parkcitymountain.com

The Canyons
4000 The Canyons Resort Drive
Park City, UT 84098
Tel. 435-649-5400
Toll-Free 888-CANYONS
Fax. 435-649-7374
www.thecanyons.com

Perhaps in an effort to encourage you to take a break, coupons for discounted lift passes, lessons, and equipment rentals for all three resorts are available to festival ticket package and pass holders. These coupons save you 20 percent at any of the three local resorts. For more information, check the Sundance Film Festival registration kit or the Web site. Or drop into one of the festival box offices or ask at the resorts themselves.

Information on skiing in Park City is also available at the visitor bureau Web site, www.parkcityinfo.com.

Please note that snowboarding is not allowed at Deer Valley, but both The Canyons and Park City Mountain Resort are happy to host snowboarders.

Cross-Country
If a well-manicured slope is not your style of skiing, a range of cross-country options are available as well. Park City is home to an assortment of companies offering cross-country skiing and training for all experience levels.

Homestead Resort
700 North Homestead Drive
Midway, UT 84049
Tel. Toll-Free 888-327-7220
www.homesteadresort.com

White Pine Cross-Country Ski Area
Corner of Park Avenue and Thaynes Canyon Drive
Park City, UT 84060
Tel. 435-649-6249
www.whitepinetouring.com

For the ultimate cross-country experience, the Norwegian Outdoor Exploration Center (Tel. 435-649-5322) offers custom-designed expeditions and tours for groups of most sizes.

Museums
Park City and the surrounding area are steeped in history, and the region boasts several excellent museums where you can find out more.

Park City Museum and Territorial Jail
Located in Park City's old 1885 City Hall, the museum offers exhibits on mining and skiing history and a restored original pioneer stagecoach.

538 Main Street
Tel. 435-649-6104
www.parkcityhistory.org

Alf Engen Ski Museum

Named after a famed Norwegian ski jumper and the director of the Alta ski school for many years, the museum features interactive exhibits depicting the history of skiing in the Wasatch Mountains, a virtual-reality ski theatre, and a 2002 Olympic gallery. It is located at the Utah Olympic Park between Kimball Junction and Park City.

3000 Bear Hollow Drive
Tel. 435-658-4236
www.engenmuseum.org

Walking

A bit of fresh mountain air can be just the thing to recharge you after a heavy night. Even if you're not skiing, you can still use the chairlifts to take a trip up one of the mountains that surround Park City. Snowshoeing is also popular, and many of the resorts and cross-country venues also offer expeditions for all levels of experience.

Hot-Air Ballooning

For a completely different perspective on Park City, you can take to the skies in a hot-air balloon. Watch the intensity of the festival fade away as you casually drift above some of the most amazing mountain landscapes in America. There are two ballooning companies in Park City:

Morning Star Balloons
Tel. 435-645-7433
www.morningstarballoons.com

Park City Balloon Adventures

P.O. Box 1344
Park City, UT 84060
Tel. 435-645-8787
Toll-Free 800-396-8787
www.pcballoonadventures.com

Ten-Pin Bowling

For an entirely non-Park City experience, jump in a car and head about 20 minutes down the road to the Heber City Bowling Alley. You can knock back a few frames and enjoy what are reputedly some of the best burgers in the area (at prices which wouldn't even cover the tip at some places in Park City). To get there, take Highway 248 (Kearns Boulevard) east out of Park City until you hit the junction with Highway 40 (Quinn's Junction, the first major intersection you come to), then follow the signs south to Heber City. The bowling alley is on the right (North Main Street) as you come into town.

Just Going for a Drive

The state of Utah is home to some amazing landscapes, and the Wasatch Mountains are definitely up there with the best of them. The scenery in and around Park City is quite impressive, but head east or south out of town, and the mountains get bigger, the crowds disappear, and you can really appreciate the spectacular sights the region has to offer. Take Highway 40 south toward Heber City, or Highway 248 east toward Kamas for some great scenery, or do a little exploring of your own.

the
festival

"You get here to Sundance, and you realise that the year and a half you pumped into your little low-budget film was not in vain. People *do* care. People *do* hear what you want to say."

Edward Burns
Actor and Director
The Brothers McMullen

"The quality of the movies is the only reason I keep coming back."

Susan Saks,
Festival Regular

the festival

Having acquired an almost-mythical status amongst many filmmakers, the Sundance Film Festival is perhaps best known as the flagship of the American independent film resurgence in the 1990s. Although the event has also gained some notoriety for hyperactive press people and staggering acquisition deals, behind these so-called excesses is a film festival which, in the face of explosive growth and a good deal of unjustified criticism, has steadfastly managed to retain its focus on two of the most important things in a film festival: the filmmakers and the audience.

Sundance has come a long way since taking its first bow in 1978 as the Utah/US Film Festival. Not only has it survived a host of adversities from debt to internal politics, hypercritical press, and the fact that it's based in a part of America which is not renowned as a hotbed of film-industry activity, but Sundance has managed to thrive and take its place on the world stage alongside a select group of festivals, most of which are more than twice its age.

Regardless of the myths and hype, the Sundance of today still feels very much like a real film festival. The program remains centred on discovery, and the festival has managed to resist intense industry pressure to refocus its competition sections on studio or star-driven films. Much of this feeling also stems from the egalitarian nature of the screenings: filmmakers and festivalgoers attend the same movies, and the post show Q&A sessions offer fans a real chance to engage with the filmmaker on a level not possible at most other events. The lack of in-your-face commerciality found at many other large festivals is also a refreshing change; those attending outside the publicity, sales, or acquisition sectors find that Sundance has a fairly leisurely pace and friendliness which is unparalleled at events of similar stature. There are no red carpets, no tuxedos, and no limos (although you ain't seen nothing until you've seen a stretch SUV). The king of American film festivals certainly deserves its crown.

history

Second only to the myth that the festival gets its name from a town called Sundance is the myth that Robert Redford started the event. Certainly Redford was involved from the very beginning, and he and the Sundance Institute are largely responsible for nurturing the event from relative obscurity to its current status as one of the top film festivals in the world. But the true origins of the festival are rooted in the collision between the state of Utah's arts and commercial needs and even predate the foundation of the Sundance Institute.

On the arts side, there was Sterling van Wagenen, a Brigham Young University film school graduate; on the commercial side, Utah State Film Commissioner John Earle. Together with a small group of associates, they decided that it would be an excellent idea to launch a film festival for the state: the Utah/US Film Festival. Van Wagenen's and Earle's vision for the festival was threefold: firstly, to hold a national event which would attract more filmmakers to Utah (one of the core mandates of Earle's post); secondly, to present a retrospective of well-regarded American films, supported by high-profile panel discussions with filmmakers, critics, and others (or as former festival program director Lory Smith puts it in his book *Party in a Box*, "...to show old movies and have famous people talk about them"); and thirdly, to start a competition where films made outside the Hollywood system could be showcased in the hope of bringing them to a wider audience.

To oversee the event, the management of the fledgling festival tapped its network of friends and colleagues to put together a board of directors. A local Utah resident since the late 1960s, Robert Redford became involved as the festival board's inaugural chairman through van Wagenen; at the time, Redford was married to Van Wagenen's cousin Lola. Funding for the festival came predominantly from Earle through the Utah Film Commission, but it also relied on industry sponsors and donations from wealthy friends of those involved.

Originally, the event was simply going to be called US Film, but it quickly picked up the "film festival" mantle as the organisers started securing sponsors and films. The word "Utah" was an eleventh-hour addition, sparking minor panic amongst those charged printing the festival programs. The change was made after concerns were raised that U.S. Film Festival might suggest to local Utahans that the event was from out of town rather than home-grown.

The first Utah/US Film Festival kicked off in Salt Lake City in September 1978 with an impressive retrospective of classic films, including *Midnight Cowboy, Mean Streets, Deliverance, A Streetcar Named Desire,* and *The Sweet Smell of Success.* Having Redford's name associated with the festival helped the young team garner interest from studios and distributors who would otherwise have probably not returned their calls. In addition to the high-profile films, eight independent features from largely unknown filmmakers were screened in the inaugural competition: six competitive films and two "honourable mentions," added at the last minute.

At the close of the festival, those in attendance almost wholeheartedly agreed that the event had been a success. The crowds had turned up — with some shows attracting lines around the block — and a handful of high-profile figures from the film industry had taken part in the filmmaker discussions. Rather curiously, the independent films in competition were more successful at the box office than most of the retrospective films. However, as the dust settled on the inaugural Utah/US Film Festival, it became apparent that all was not peachy.

In their enthusiasm to get the festival off the ground, the organisers had managed to close the books on the 1978 festival with a debt to the tune of $40,000 — almost one-third of the entire budget. But ironically, this debt became one of the main factors which encouraged the festival's continued existence; creditors realised that the only possible way they could recoup their investment was through ticket sales for another event.

Planning commenced for the 1979 festival the following spring, and enough money was raised through a combination of sponsors and private donations to cover the administration costs (but not the debt). With a new retrospective slate and the independent feature film competition again featuring eight films, the 1979 festival continued where the previous year had left off. At the close of the event, ticket sales were up on the year before (once again, independent films proved to be a major drawing card), and the organisers had even managed to knock off around half of the $40,000 debt.

As the festival looked to a third outing, debt again proved to be a major factor in ensuring the young event's continued existence. Initial planning for the third Utah/US Film Festival began in March 1980; however, early in the process, director Sydney Pollack (also on the festival's board of directors) half-jokingly suggested to the management team, "You ought to move the festival to Park City and set it in the wintertime." He went on to point out that the event would be "...the only film festival in the world

held in a ski resort during ski season, and Hollywood would beat down the door to attend." Once the idea sank in, the rest of the festival board and management seemed to agree, and the 1980 festival was pushed back to January 1981. The move to Park City not only proved to be a boon for festival attendance, but shrewd planning placed the event during the third week of January, filling what was traditionally a dead period for the local tourist industry.

The third festival kicked off with a larger program of independent films than ever before; the slate reportedly expanded at the suggestion of program director Lory Smith, who pointed out that independent films were considerably cheaper to show because, unlike Hollywood films, it wasn't necessary to pay rental fees to screen them. The 1981 festival also brought another name change for the event; it became the United States Film and Video Festival. The word "video" was added because the board of directors felt it was important to be inclusive of this new visual medium, even though the festival wasn't actually able to program any videos that year.

At the time, it appeared that the third United States Film and Video Festival was a resounding success. However, after the curtain fell for the first time in Park City, it became apparent that, although many films had drawn record audiences, heavy snowfalls during the event had brought the overall attendance down. But perhaps a more worrying discovery for the festival management and directors was the fact that the event had managed to slide further into the red to the tune of about $100,000. Whilst most people involved were keen for the festival to continue, there was pressure from some factions within the organisation to abandon the focus on independent films in favour of screening more glamorous Hollywood pictures, which some believed would help attract sponsors. Fortunately, this never came to pass as financial support for the next festival was ultimately secured through the Utah Film Commission, a couple of key donors, and a line of credit with a local bank (personally signed for by the festival's board). This allowed plans to move forward for the fourth annual United States Film and Video Festival in 1982.

Park City was kind to the young event in its fourth year. The snowfalls were mercifully light, preventing the attendance problems of the previous year. The lack of snow also meant that ski-visitor numbers were significantly down, so for the first time, the locals viewed the festival as a positive thing for the town. In fact, the visitor numbers generated by the festival helped take the edge off what had otherwise been a disastrous ski season so far that year.

The 1982 festival also saw the program expand yet again. The documentary competition had its own section for the first time, a collection of short films was included, and to support the video component of the event's title, a program was added to highlight video art, video documentaries, and movies made for television (the latter was a slightly odd addition because most TV movies were shot on film at that time). All in all, the 1982 festival

ended up being the most successful to date, with box-office numbers up on previous years, significant progress toward reducing the debt, and the widest range of films screened yet. The video program, however, proved to be disappointing and was dropped for the 1984 event, even though the festival held on to its "and Video" moniker for another year.

The next two years, 1983 and 1984, proved pivotal for the festival as it firmly cemented its feet on the national film map and, more importantly, in the minds of the press. Despite extremely tight funding, the programs consistently rewarded attendees with a broad range of independent films, supported by the more glamorous premieres and retrospectives. However, debt continued to plague the festival, and after the 1984 event, dissention was rife amongst the management and the board of directors, threatening to scuttle the festival altogether.

In 1985, salvation came from amongst the festival's own, so to speak, as the event moved under the wing of the fledgling Sundance Institute for the first time. Several years before, in late 1979, many festival staff members and film associates had joined Robert Redford at his ranch to take part in a planning meeting for what became the Sundance Institute. The two organisations therefore had a natural connection from the start, and the case for Sundance taking over management of the festival seemed to be persuasive for all concerned. From the Institute's point of view, one of its key initiatives was to develop new outlets for independent films, and running a high-profile festival was clearly a powerful weapon to add to its arsenal. From the Festival's point of view, it made sense to be part of an organisation which could provide year-round staffing, financial backing, and an extensive network of contacts.

To help move the two organisations toward this holy matrimony, Utah Film Commissioner John Earle and festival program director Lory Smith convinced Sterling van Wagenen (at that point the Institute's executive director) that it would be in everyone's best interests for Sundance to take over the festival. The board of directors was initially lukewarm to the idea, but some impressive statesmanship from Earle and Smith, as well as Van Wagenen securing Redford's support for the decision, ultimately convinced it.

Under the sponsorship of the Sundance Institute, the 1985 United States Film Festival presented more than 80 features, including, for the first time, a slate of international films. The seventh festival also witnessed the arrival of the first generation of true superstars of the independent film world: the Coen brothers' debut film *Blood Simple* walked away with the Grand Jury Prize, and Jim Jarmusch's *Stranger Than Paradise* impressed the dramatic competition jury enough to earn a Special Jury Prize. Festival attendance in 1985 was also up, doubling the previous year's figures, and as part of the move to a year-round management structure, Van Wagenen appointed Tony Safford, formerly with the National Endowment for the Arts in Washington, as the new festival program director.

As the 1980s marched to a close, the festival continued to enhance its profile and attendance figures with a blend of themed collections, retrospectives, and what had become the premiere forum for independent film in the United States. Between 1986 and 1988, around 200 feature films were screened, including Woody Allen's *Hannah and Her Sisters* (1986); Tim Hunter's classic film with a young Keanu Reeves, *River's Edge* (1987); an early Robin Williams dramatic effort, *Seize the Day* (1987); Lizzie Borden's *Working Girls* (1987); cult French film *Betty Blue* (1987); and John Waters' *Hairspray* (1988). But it was 1989 that proved to be a major turning point for the festival.

Since the inaugural Utah/US Film Festival in 1978, the press attention focused on the event had increased exponentially every year. In 1989, the pressure on the festival to play breakout films was more intense than ever, and ironically, it was a former festival bus driver who ended up giving the press what they craved. In 1988, Steven Soderbergh had spent two weeks in Park City ferrying festivalgoers around town as a volunteer driver. Returning in 1989 with his debut film *sex, lies and videotape*, he not only won the inaugural Audience Award but sparked a studio bidding war and hype machine that eventually earned the film over $25 million at the U.S. box office and, in the process, cemented the festival's reputation as an essential calendar date for the U.S. film industry. If the press wanted "break-out," they weren't disappointed.

But the success of *sex, lies and videotape* wasn't the only highlight in 1989. With 65 other feature films, including Michael Lehmann's *Heathers*, Martin Donovan's *Apartment Zero*, and Nancy Savoca's *True Love*, which won the Grand Jury Prize, as well as a 15-film tribute to John Cassavetes and a centennial celebration of the work of Charlie Chaplin, the 1989 event offered a host of treats for festivalgoers.

The success of the previous year created extremely high expectations for the 1990 festival, and although it didn't deliver quite the same level of hype, the event managed to maintain the impressive breadth and depth of the film offerings. Highlights in 1990 included Michael Moore's biting documentary *Roger & Me*, Hal Hartley's *The Unbelievable Truth*, Jane Campion's *Sweetie*, and Reginald Hudlin's *House Party*, as well as programs of films from Colombia and Kazakhstan, and tributes to directors Richard Lester (*A Hard Day's Night, How I Won the War, Robin and Marian*) and Melvin van Peebles (*The Story of a Three-Day Pass, Watermelon Man, Sweet Sweetback's Baadasssss Song*). That year also saw yet-another tweak to the festival's name: the event bowed as the slightly awkward Sundance/United States Film Festival.

The arrival of 1991 bought a range of changes both at the festival and in the wider world. Against the backdrop of hostilities commencing in the first Gulf War, the Sundance Institute quietly celebrated its 10th anniversary, current festival honcho Geoffrey Gilmore took over the programming reins from Tony Safford, and the event registered its final name change,

becoming simply the Sundance Film Festival. Highlights of 1991 included Lasse Hallstrom's *Once Around*, Hal Hartley's *Trust*, Todd Haynes' *Poison*, which won the Grand Jury Prize, John Sayles' *City of Hope*, Stephen Frears' *The Grifters*, and Richard Linklater's *Slacker* (the first of a spectrum of films over the next few years which would become synonymous with the festival and independent film in America). In addition to a strong dramatic slate, the 1991 festival also premiered a wide selection of documentaries, dipped its hat to Robert Altman and British director Michael Powell, and presented a special program focused on Japanese cinema.

As the '90s moved up a gear, interest in independent film experienced explosive growth, and the Sundance Film Festival was fast becoming the flagship of the new movement. The 1992 festival delivered an expanded program of the best films from American and international independent filmmakers, in addition to some of the most notorious ones. The biggest splash was of course made by struggling actor and former video-store clerk Quentin Tarantino, who presented his debut feature, the ultra-violent *Reservoir Dogs*. But 1992 also unleashed a number of other strong films, including Allison Anders's *Gas, Food Lodging*, Neal Jimenez and Michael Steinberg's *The Waterdance*, Mira Nair's *Mississippi Masala*, and Errol Morris' remarkable documentary on wheelchair-bound physics genius Stephen Hawking, *A Brief History of Time*. Tribute programs also celebrated the work of Stanley Kubrick and Chinese director Zhang Yimou (*Ju Dou, Raise the Red Lantern,*

Yellow Earth), and John Turturro became the inaugural recipient of the Tribute to Independent Vision.

The 1993 festival pretty much picked up where the previous year left off, screening 80 feature films and more than 60 shorts and setting a new attendance record of 55,000 tickets sold. Some of the more memorable films included Sally Potter's *Orlando*, Bryan Singer's *Public Access*, Alfonso Arau's *Like Water for Chocolate*, and Victor Nunez's *Ruby in Paradise* (co-winner with *Public Access* of the Grand Jury Prize). Two other films also captured the spotlight in 1993, albeit for entirely different reasons. The first was Robert Rodriguez's *El Mariachi*, which not only picked up the Audience Award, but the story of how he made the film for $7,000 became instrumental in pushing the DIY filmmaking movement into full bloom. The other film that attracted a lot of attention in 1993 was Jennifer (daughter of David) Lynch's *Boxing Helena*, which outraged critics and audiences alike for its macabre subject matter.

That year, festival regulars also began to notice how much the business side of the event influenced those who made the trek to Park City. In his festival wrap in Newsweek, journalist David Ansen noted, "It was an irritating but not uncommon sight at the 1993 Sundance Film Festival; a guy in a movie theatre, whispering into his cellular phone as the lights go down." Ansen went on to comment, "Agents and lawyers were crawling all over the snowy streets of Park City, Utah, this year; it was said William Morris Agency alone had 25 reps in place, scouring the festival for the next breakthrough twenty-something filmmaker... [The festival] has become a tension-filled auction block, with long waiting lists for the hot screenings and nervous young filmmakers whose futures are on the line." And it would take another seven festivals for things to calm down a little.

Sundance 1994 kicked off with one of the most bumper crops of conspicuous films the event had ever seen. The line-up of more than 90 features included Ben Stiller's *Reality Bites*, Rose Troche's *Go Fish*, John Duigan's *Sirens*, Mike Newell's *Four Weddings and a Funeral*, Scott McGehee and David Siegel's *Suture*, and David O. Russell's *Spanking the Monkey*, although in what has become something of a Sundance tradition, the lion's share of the awards went to films with much lower profiles. The 1994 festival also featured the first look at Steve James' amazing documentary *Hoop Dreams* (winner of the Audience Award), saluted the work of director Arthur Penn (*Bonnie and Clyde, Alice's Restaurant*), and marked the arrival of Kevin Smith on the scene with his seminal DIY film *Clerks* (which was awarded the peer-voted Filmmakers Trophy). The massive increase in film submissions for the 1994 event (and resultant lower selection success rate) also gave birth to the first of the now plentiful alternative festivals — Slamdance.

For the 1995 outing, the number of films in the program increased yet again, this time to more than 100 feature films and 70 shorts. The bulk of the heavy publicity machine focused on Ed Burns and his debut film *The Brothers McMullen* (winner of the Grand Jury Prize). However, the rest of the line-up was as strong as ever, with diverse films such as Antonia Bird's *Priest*, Atom Egoyan's *Exotica*, Richard Linklater's *Before Sunrise*, Abel Ferrara's *The Addiction*, Tom DiCillo's *Living in Oblivion*, and James Mangold's *Heavy*. The festival also presented special sidebars focused on world cinema, personal documentaries, animation, and Native American film, and bestowed the Tribute to Independent Vision on Nicolas Cage.

With the independent film renaissance in full swing and Sundance firmly in the centre of it, the 1996 festival bowed to record crowds (approximately 10,000 attendees) and the largest slate of films to date. Another record set during that year was the sum of money spent by acquisition executives to get their mitts on the next *Clerks* or *The Brothers McMullen*. Indeed the acquisition activity during the festival was getting so cutthroat that it often spilled over into open argument; one infamous incident involved Miramax boss Harvey Weinstein and Pandora Cinema's Jonathan Taplin engaging in a public shouting match in a Park City restaurant over which company had actually closed the deal for the Australian movie *Shine*. And all of this against the backdrop of one of the heaviest Park City snowfalls during the festival in many years (10 feet in 10 days). Memorable films in 1996 included the Campbell Scott/Stanley Tucci co-directed *Big Night*, Mary Harron's *I Shot Andy Warhol*, Todd Solondz's *Welcome to the Dollhouse*, which won the Grand Jury Prize, Lee David Zlotoff's Audience Award winner *Care of the Spitfire Grill*, and

Leon Gast's documentary on the Muhammad Ali/George Foreman fight, *When We Were Kings*.

The 1997 festival brought with it something of a "market correction" in terms of business deals. A more sober approach to acquisitions became the norm following poor box-office performance by most of the previous year's buzz films. But this didn't dampen the quality of the festival itself, which featured another impressive line-up of films, including many from amongst Sundance alumni like Errol Morris, Tom DiCillo, Victor Nunez, and Kevin Smith, as well as a major retrospective of the work of German new-wave giant Rainer Werner Fassbinder.

With another record attendance in 1997, Sundance was literally bulging at the seams. Problems with venue sizes and public transportation — not to mention the fact that it had become common for the entire telephone system in Park City to crash on a regular basis under the massive load — began to highlight a question the festival hadn't had to face before: Was the event getting too big for Park City to handle? A few voices suggested that the festival should move back to Salt Lake City to provide better facilities for an event that size. Vehement opposition to a move, however, came from Park City itself; businesses and local officials were unwilling to give up an event which by now generated around $20 million of direct investment into the town each year.

Sundance 1998 went ahead in Park City as planned, the solution to overcrowding woes coming in the form of a more streamlined approach to the event's organisation and the completion of the 1,300-seat Eccles Center, which alleviated the crunch in screening space. The crowds were still there — the Park Record's Tom Clyde noted that the town was full of "people with a clear vision for film, but only a vague notion of winter at 7,000 feet" — and the phone network still crashed from time to time, but that didn't seem to bother most festival attendees, who were there simply to enjoy the films. The telephone system was eventually beefed up for the Winter Olympics in 2002.

The films in 1998 included Vincent Gallo's debut *Buffalo 66*, Don Roos' *The Opposite of Sex*, David Mamet's *The Spanish Prisoner*, Peter Howitt's *Sliding Doors*, and Darren Aronofsky's *Pi*. Controversy also surrounded Nick Broomfield's documentary *Kurt and Courtney*, which was dropped from the festival in the face of legal threats by Courtney Love, allegedly over music rights. Slamdance also decided to pass, so perhaps with less to lose (and more to gain) than the others, upstart alternative festival Slamdunk agreed to screen the film. The lawsuit never materialised.

If the charge levelled by some that Sundance in the '90s had become more about the hype than the films is to be believed, then it was fitting that the 1999 festival bought a climax to the excitement that had never been witnessed before and has never been repeated. While the festival quietly celebrated its 21st anniversary, *Blair Witch* mania broke out of the fabled midnight screenings, and the film went on to become the most successful independent release of all

time, grossing more than $140 million in the U.S. alone. If *El Mariachi* had revitalised the DIY filmmaking ethic six years before, the success of *The Blair Witch Project* dragged it fully into the spotlight. But the 1999 festival went beyond the hype surrounding *Blair Witch*. Doug Liman also presented *Go*, his follow-up to indie hit *Swingers*, and the German film *Run Lola Run* went down well with festivalgoers, bagging the World Cinema Audience Award.

With the turn of the new millennium, the relentless hype machine that surrounded the Sundance Film Festival in the 1990s seemed to have finally run out of steam. It was going to be very difficult to match the excitement of the 1999 event, and instead of trying, the festival showed its maturity with a move back in the direction of its roots — concentrating more on the films than the hype surrounding them. Many of the memorable films in the 2000 program focused on strong character-driven stories, including Miguel Arteta's *Chuck & Buck*, Karyn Kusama's *Girlfight*, which won the Grand Jury Prize, Kenneth Lonergan's *You Can Count on Me*, and Jenniphr Goodman's *The Tao of Steve*. Kevin Spacey was also honoured at the 2000 festival with the Tribute to Independent Vision.

The 11th festival under the Sundance moniker continued along the path laid down the previous year. The hype was kept under control, and the 2001 event focused firmly on the films and filmmakers. Christopher Nolan's striking debut *Memento* was a treat for festival audiences, but a number of other films were also well received, including Scott McGehee and

David Siegel's *The Deep End*, John Cameron Mitchell's *Hedwig and the Angry Inch*, Henry Bean's *The Believer*, which won the Grand Jury Prize, and Todd Field's *In the Bedroom* (which earned several Academy Award nominations later in the year). On the documentary side, Stacy Peralta's ode to the skateboarding days of his friends' youth, *Dogtown and Z-Boys*, also made a splash (picking up the Audience Award), and in recognition of the independent spirit in filmmakers who were producing works for online distribution, the first Sundance Online Film Festival hit the Web.

In February 2002, the juggernaut that is the Winter Olympic Games rolled into Park City, and Sundance kicked off early to make room for the massive event. Although Salt Lake City was the official Olympic host, more than a third of the events were held in the Park City area. Perhaps spurred on by the size of the upcoming event, the 2002 festival presented a record 120 feature films to eager audiences, in addition to one of the widest selections of non-film events (such as panels and music performances) seen in Park City for years. Memorable films included Gary Winick's *Tadpole*, Rebecca Miller's *Personal Velocity*, which won the Grand Jury Prize, and Patricia Cardoso's crowd pleaser, *Real Women Have Curves* (unsurprisingly the dramatic Audience Award winner).

After all the excitement in Park City in 2002, most people would have been fairly forgiving if the festival had taken it easy the following year. However staying true to form, Sundance 2003 continued on its steady course of discovery. With the mildest weather in recent memory (almost no snow at all fell during the festival), a record crowd of over 38,000 visitors enjoyed a bumper crop of 250 films. Among the highlights were Tom McCarthy's *The Station Agent*, Shari Springer-Berman and Robert Pulcini's Grand Jury Prize winning *American Splendour*, and Andrew Jarecki's fascinating documentary, *Capturing the Friedmans*, which focussed on a middle-class family whose obsession with videoing themselves is interrupted when the father and youngest son are arrested on child molestation charges. The World Cinema program also presented some strong offerings, particularly Niki Caro's popular *Whale Rider*, which unsurprisingly, bagged the coveted World Cinema Audience award. Another notable fact in 2003 was just how much digital video had taken over as the medium of choice for independent filmmakers. Nearly 50 feature films (including all, but one of the 16 documentaries) were shot on digital video, compared to only 13 just two years before.

The line-up for the 2004 festival marked a notably return to traditional Sundance territory, with a string of low-budget films showcasing quirky characters, clever screenplays, and alternative visions. It was suggested in some circles that 2004 was perhaps the most low-key festival in more than a decade. However, Newmarket Films boss Bob Berney was probably closer to the mark when he suggested that it was simply because the event was "... more focussed on the films, instead of the people and the parties" (a reference also, to the number of column inches generated the previous year by the presence of non-affiliated celebrities such as Jennifer Lopez and Britney Spears).

On the film side of things, the festival curtain was raised for the first time in Park City (historically the opening night took place in Salt Lake City) with the sophomore effort from Stacey Peralta, *Riding Giants*. Peralta's follow-up to 2001's *Dogtown & Z-Boys*, this time centred on surfing, was not only the first non-dramatic film ever to open the festival, it was also one of a record haul of over 40-odd documentaries screened during Sundance 2004. Other notable films in the program included the US premiere of Walter Salles' *The Motorcycle Diaries*, based on the journals of Cuban revolutionary (and student pin-up) Ché Guevara; Shane Carruth's *Primer* (winner of the dramatic Grand Jury Prize); Ondi Timoner's *DiG!*, shot over seven years and chronicling the friendship/rivalry between two rock bands; Audience Award winners *Maria Full of Grace* (Joshua Marston) and *Seducing Doctor Lewis* (Jean-François Pouilot); and Morgan Spurlock's *Super Size Me*, an eye-opening piece documenting his gruelling experiment of surviving for 30 days on nothing but McDonalds fastfood.

Today, the Sundance Film Festival continues to be the pre-eminent event of its type in America and is considered one of the top five film festivals in the world (alongside Cannes, Venice, Toronto, and Berlin). Although the arrival of the new millennium has bought fresh challenges for the festival management, such as overzealous, non-affiliated corporate brands attempting to cash in on the publicity, and an increasingly blurred line between studio and independent films, the festival remains firmly focused on showcasing the talents of America's independent filmmakers. Sundance is also trying to position itself to become, according to current director Geoffrey Gilmore, a "launch pad for English-language films." The festival continues to set attendance records (nearly 40,000 visitors in 2004), and submissions remain as high as ever (more than 5,870 in 2004) as the next generation of filmmakers try hard to get a piece of the Sundance dream.

festival structure

The astronomical growth experienced by the festival during the 1990s created a need to expand the number of films screened and introduce more effective ways of grouping them together for easy digestion by the audience. Today, no less than nine separate sections make up the Sundance Film Festival program. These are the following:

Independent Feature Film Competition
Many consider this to be the main event at Sundance, and consequently, films in this program tend to get the lion's share of acquisitions and media attention. Within the Independent Feature Film Competition are two categories — one for dramatic features and one for documentaries — and around 16 films compete in each for a variety of awards. The Independent Feature Film Competition is restricted to independent American films.

American Spectrum

In an effort to address concerns that the festival's focus on American independent cinema was becoming diluted through an expanded program of international films, American Spectrum was added to the program in 1996. A non-competitive section, American Spectrum aims to survey the landscape of America's most promising new independent filmmakers and promote their work to a wider audience. American Spectrum includes both dramatic and documentary films, and the films are eligible for the Audience Awards.

Frontier

Since its early days as the Utah/US Film Festival, Sundance has provided a forum for experimental films that push the boundaries of cinema. Frontier is the banner under which such films now play in the festival program. Frontier is open to films of all types and lengths, from any country.

World Cinema

Although historically the Sundance Film Festival has celebrated the best of American independent film, international cinema now plays an increasingly prominent role in the event. From 2005 onwards, World Cinema will be a competitive event, championing international films with independent spirit for American audiences. As with the Independent Feature Film Competition, the World Cinema Competition is separated into two categories; one for dramatic films and one for documentaries. Approximately 28 films are selected (16 features and 12 documentaries), and a jury prize is awarded to the best film in each category. World Cinema is open to dramatic feature films made outside the United States.

Park City at Midnight

Perhaps the most notorious Sundance program, Park City at Midnight has long had a reputation for screening films guaranteed to provoke a reaction. Historically, tremendously diverse films that range across many genres and subject matters have occupied these screening slots. The "rags to riches" success story of *The Blair Witch Project* has its roots in the buzz generated from its midnight screenings during the 1999 festival, but the program has also served up over-the-top comedies, international hits, surreal drama, and animation for late-night audiences. As the festival itself suggests, Park City at Midnight is "a good place to find a new cult classic."

Premieres

This is a showcase program for new films from respected American and international directors. Films in the Premieres program usually have theatrical distribution in place, but are invited to take part in the festival on the basis of their compelling stories or innovative approaches.

Shorts

Short filmmaking has always been a proving ground for new talent and a test bed for groundbreaking approaches to storytelling. The Sundance Film Festival Shorts program recognises this talent and experimentation by bringing these films to a wider audience. Sundance shorts are either shown before a main feature or grouped together into feature-length programs. The Shorts program is open to films from all countries.

From the Sundance Collection
One of the Sundance Institute's major activities is the collection and preservation of independent films for future generations. The fruits of this labour are manifested in the Sundance Collection, housed in Los Angeles at the UCLA Film and Television Archive. During the festival, a selection of treasures from Sundance's archive are presented alongside the regular programs to give festivalgoers a chance to contrast the current landscape of independent filmmaking against a selection of important works from the past.

Special Screenings
Each year, the Sundance Film Festival also presents a program of special screenings. These range from retrospectives of influential filmmakers' work to groups of films from countries with low cinematic visibility, and to interesting films that evade classification in existing festival programs.

other festival events

In addition to the film programs, Sundance presents a variety of other events for the enjoyment of festivalgoers each year. Some of these events are permanent fixtures in the Sundance calendar, whilst others vary from year to year. The Sundance events program is usually announced in mid-December, but in practice, it's not unusual for events to be added right up to the opening day of the festival. To get the full rundown on events for the upcoming year, see the official festival film guide or visit the Web site (www.sundance.org).

Panel Discussions
Complementing the screening program, panel discussions have been one of the main attractions of the event since the inaugural Utah/US Film Festival in 1978. Panel discussions involve groups of people from every corner of the film industry, brought together for presentations, informal conversations, and lively debates on issues that cut across the entire filmmaking landscape. The panel discussions are all ticketed events and use the same system as the films. Since many of the panels involve high-profile speakers, places fill up fast, so you'll need to book early.

Filmmaker Lodge
Aside from being a great venue for laid-back networking, the Filmmaker Lodge also hosts a selection of other events for festivalgoers. These include a series of panels centred on documentary and dramatic filmmaking issues, and informal gatherings where filmmakers have the opportunity to meet members of the national and international press. The schedule for the Filmmaker Lodge is usually announced in mid-December.

Sundance Digital Center
In recognition of the impact digital technologies are having on the world of filmmaking, the Sundance Digital Center provides a series of exhibits and seminars covering issues related to technology and filmmaking. Forums and exhibits are free and

open to all, although you will need to get there early to ensure a seat for some seminars. The seminar program and exhibitor list is usually announced in mid-December. In addition, the Digital Centre is also the place where the Sundance Online Film Festival meets the real world. It houses a dedicated screening room and a collection of media PCs which allow you to explore the online festival at your own pace.

Sundance Music Café
During the day, the Sundance Music Café hosts free performances from a range of new and established artists. Daytime events are open to all festival credential holders on a first-come, first-served basis.

The daytime programs for the Sundance Music Café are usually announced in mid-December; however, like many other events, the schedule is tweaked right up until the last minute. Since it's not possible to book for music café events, it's advisable to get there early, particularly for performances by big-name artists or other highly anticipated gigs.

Sundance Online Film Festival
Launched at the turn of the new millennium, the Sundance Online Film Festival is not only your free ticket to all of the short films screening in Park City during the festival, but gives you exclusive access to behind the scenes interviews with festival filmmakers. Starting in 2005, the Sundance Online Film Festival also includes a special Frontier section - a dedicated program of cutting edge work in experimental media created just for the Web.

The Sundance Online Film Festival usually begins screening at www.sundance.org on the first day of the festival. In Park City itself, the online festival has its own screening room in the Sundance Digital Center. Here films can be viewed, and Q&A sessions are held where the filmmakers discuss their work.

submission and selection

With Sundance now standing shoulder to shoulder with the world's best festivals, the number of films submitted for consideration gets higher each year. Whilst the original Utah/US Film Festival struggled to get 36 entries for the Independent Feature Film Competition, Sundance now receives well over 5,500 submissions each year. Out of that number, only about 4 percent of films make it into one of the official programs. The overall program is usually broken down into 16 American dramatic features and 16 American documentaries for the Independent Feature Film Competition, and 16 international dramatic and 12 international documentaries for the World Cinema Competition; the rest is made up of shorts, showcases, and special screenings. As you can imagine, competition for a festival berth is extremely fierce.

Submitting Your Film
Submitting your film for Sundance consideration is a straightforward and painless process. It isn't necessary to be a sales agent or distributor, nor do you need to have any form of professional representation. Although a good sales agent and/ or publicist may be able to offer

some advice on how to prepare your submission, Sundance doesn't respond to pitches, and elaborate press materials are largely a waste of time. The chance of landing a Sundance berth ultimately rests on the film itself.

As you can imagine, however, a few criteria must be met to make a film eligible for selection. These are the following:

Language
For a film to be considered for Sundance, it must either be in English or have English subtitles. All costs associated with subtitling are the responsibility of the producer or other appropriate representative of the film.

Running Time
A film is considered to be a short if its running time is less than 70 minutes for a dramatic film or 50 minutes for a documentary. Films with longer running times are considered features.

Completion Dates
To be eligible for Sundance, all feature films must have been completed no earlier than 14 months before the festival for U.S. films, or 12 months before the festival in the case of international films. For shorts and online projects, the festival also prefers a completion date 12 months before the festival; however, exceptions have been made in the past for outstanding works.

Prior Screenings
As one of the top film festivals in the world, Sundance prefers that all films submitted either have their world premiere, or at least their U.S. premiere, in Park City. For a film to be considered for the Independent Feature Film Competition (in either the dramatic or documentary strand), a world premiere is mandatory. In the case of the World Cinema Competition, all films must have at least their U.S. premiere at Sundance, however the festival does give special consideration to international films which will have their world premiere in Park City.

All films submitted must also not have had a theatrical release or be broadcast in any format (including over the Internet) in the U.S. prior to the beginning of the February following the festival.

Financing
Films submitted to Sundance must not be produced, financed, or initiated by a major motion picture studio. However, films produced, financed, or acquired by an independent division of a studio are eligible. To be considered for the Independent Feature Film competition or American Spectrum, a film must have at least 51 percent U.S. financing.

Screening Prints
If a film is selected for the festival, either a print must be made available (16mm or 35mm) or the film must be delivered in an approved digital format (usually Sony HDCAM, but always confirm with the festival). Film prints must be composite prints with the soundtrack and titles included. The festival does not screen other types of prints (for example, double-

head, super 16, etc). All printing and/or format conversion costs must be paid by the film's producer or other representative.

Submission Process

To submit your film for consideration, you need to jump online and point your Web browser to the Sundance Institute Web site (www.sundance. org). Once you're there, complete the online entry form as directed and pay your entry fee with a credit or debit card. Entry fees vary from year to year but are always displayed on the Web site along with the entry forms and other relevant information. As a rough guide, the fee to submit a feature film is around $50, and for a short, $35.

The entry form is pretty straightforward and includes detailed guidance within most sections. When submitting your film, it isn't necessary to specify which festival program you are applying for; festival programmers will view your film and, if it is selected, place it in the program they feel is most appropriate. Berths in the Premiere program are by invitation only.

After you submit your online application form, you will receive a unique reference number. Include this with the following materials, which you need to send to the festival:

A Copy of Your Film

Copies should be sent on standard VHS or DVD only. The festival doesn't accept any other formats (that means no SVHS, MiniDV, DVCAM, HDCAM, DigiBeta, BetaSP, Umatic, film prints, streaming media, zoetropes, etc). Submitted tapes and discs can be in either PAL or NTSC, but remember to label clearly your tape or disc format.

If you're planning on submitting your film on DVD, it's advisable to read the festival's DVD Submission FAQ very carefully. With consumer DVD-burning technology still in relative infancy, there are many considerations to ensure that the Sundance programmers have a smooth viewing experience (and subsequently enhance the chances of your film being selected). The full DVD Submission FAQ is available at the Web site (www.sundance.org), but these are the key points:

- DVDs should either be Region 0 (unlocked) or Region 1 (North America) because the festival cannot play DVDs from other regions.

- DVDs should be submitted in standard plastic DVD cases (5¼ x 7½ inch / 133 x 190mm) — don't waste time and/or money on fancy cases as they will just get binned.

- DVDs should be in standard format; in other words, MPEG-2 files formatted for playback on a DVD player. For maximum compatibility, you should probably author your DVD using DVD-R media. The festival doesn't accept data DVDs (i.e., those formatted for a computer) containing MPEG-1, Windows Media, Quicktime, or any other digital media files.

If you're using your own burner to author your DVD submission, make sure you test your disc in as many non-computer DVD players as possible. Burnt DVDs are notoriously troublesome in regular players, and it would be a shame to miss out on a Sundance berth simply because your burnt disc isn't compatible with the festival's DVD player.

In years gone by, the festival was quite open to arranging a selection screening for films with an available print. However, the sheer volume of submissions the festival now receives has unfortunately forced this practice to be discontinued. Regardless of whether you have a print available, you still need to submit a VHS or DVD copy of your film.

An Iconic Still

When you shot your film, you should have also taken as many still photographs of your characters as possible. Now is the time to choose the most iconic still you have, one which best sums up your film in a single frame. If your film is selected, this photograph will appear in the festival film guide and catalogue along with the descriptive capsule, and we all know how many words an iconic picture speaks...

Stills should be 8 x 10 inches (203 x 254mm) or smaller and can be in colour or black and white. The still should show scenes and/or characters from your film (not the director looking cool or artistic or the group photo from your wrap party). The festival prefers that you submit your still as a print; however, transparencies and high-resolution digital files are also acceptable. If you're thinking of submitting digitally, make sure your image is around 300dpi and the print size is

as close to 8 x 10 as you can get (if you don't know how to check image dpi and print sizes, you should probably submit a print or transparency instead).

Once you've got your materials together, make sure they're all clearly labelled with your film's title, director, and contact details (at minimum a phone number or email address), then send your package to this address:

Sundance Film Festival
Film ID #
8857 West Olympic Boulevard
Suite 200
Beverly Hills, CA 90211-3605
U.S.A.

(Film ID is the unique reference number generated by the online application form.)

You can submit as many films as you like for Sundance consideration so long as they all meet the festival criteria. You do, however, need to complete a separate entry form for each one, pay the appropriate fee, and submit each film on its own tape or DVD. The festival does not accept multiple submissions on the same media.

As you can imagine, with more than 5,500 submissions each year, the festival unfortunately cannot confirm receipt of individual entries. It therefore recommends that you send your materials via registered or certified mail to ensure they are delivered safely and on time. Alternatively, you can include a stamped, self-addressed postcard with your submission, which the festival will then send back to you as confirmation.

If the completion of your film is imminent, but won't happen in time for the deadline, the festival is happy to accept a rough cut for initial consideration (obviously, you should only submit a rough cut if your film will definitely be finished in time for the event). If you do decide to submit a work in progress or an edit with temporary music, clearly outline on the tape box or DVD sleeve which elements are missing. If your film receives a festival berth, it will be conditional on the missing elements being completed in time for the film's first festival screening.

Films which were submitted for a previous Sundance Film Festival, but weren't selected, are generally not eligible for resubmission unless they have been substantial reediting or significantly changed (and, of course, the film must still meet all the selection criteria). If you do decide to resubmit your film, you must include detailed information in your supporting materials describing the changes that have been made.

The Sundance Web site (www. sundance.org) also includes a detailed Film Submissions FAQ (list of frequently asked questions), which you should review before completing the application form or contacting the festival. If after reading the information in the FAQ, you still have questions, contact Sundance at the Los Angeles office at 310-360-1981 or via email to programming@sundance.org.

Dates and Deadlines

The Sundance Film Festival usually puts out its first call for entries at the beginning of June each year. To encourage early submission (and thereby reduce the administrative nightmare caused by the last-minute rush), the festival offers discounted fees for entries received within the first two months of the call being announced. Only completed films are eligible for early submission (no rough cuts or works in progress), and the entry fees revert to full price at the beginning of August.

The deadline for final submission is dependent on the type of film:

International Short Films
Mid-August

American Short Films
Mid-September

All Feature Films
Beginning of October

The exact cut-off dates vary from year to year, so you should always check the Sundance Web site (www. sundance.org) to get the relevant dates for the next festival. It's also worth noting that all deadlines are the date by which the festival must have received your submission and not the postmark date (i.e., the date when you sent it).

If you're lucky (and talented) enough to have your film selected, you will be contacted with the good news in late November. At the end of November, the Sundance Institute issues a press release announcing the slate of films chosen for the next festival. This list is available on the Web site, but considering the profile of the event, it also appears in all the industry trade magazines almost immediately.

Again, due to the sheer volume of submissions, the festival only notifies successful entries and sadly cannot provide any feedback on films that don't make the cut.

Sundance Online Film Festival

In previous years, the Sundance Online Film Festival had its own submission procedure. Now films submitted through the normal channels are also considered for the online festival.

juries and awards

Although Sundance is primarily about showcasing the work of independent filmmakers, the festival includes a competitive program where films vie for a number of awards, and films in several other programs outside the actual competition also qualify for certain awards. The responsibility for picking the award winners from the remainder of the festival crop is divided amongst seven juries. Jury members are selected by the festival from the length and breadth of the American and international film industries on the basis of their status as an artist and their independent vision.

Dramatic Competition Jury

This jury scrutinises the dramatic films in the Independent Feature Film Competition and bestows the following awards:

Grand Jury Prize

The daddy of all Sundance awards,

the Grand Jury Prize is presented to the film the jury feels is the best dramatic film of the competition.

Directing Award

Presented to the dramatic film which the jury believes represents the best achievement in directing.

Excellence in Cinematography

Awarded by the jury to the dramatic film which has the most outstanding cinematography.

Waldo Salt Screenwriting Award

Named for the Academy Award–winning screenwriter of *The Philadelphia Story*, *Midnight Cowboy*, *Serpico*, and *Coming Home*, this award honours the most outstanding screenplay amongst the dramatic competition films. Both original and adapted screenplays are eligible for the Waldo Salt Screenwriting Award.

Documentary Competition Jury

The Documentary Competition Jury examines the documentary films in the Independent Feature Film Competition and bestows the following awards:

Grand Jury Prize

As with the dramatic films, the jury awards the Grand Jury Prize to the film they feel is the best documentary of the competition.

Directing Award

Presented to the documentary film which the jury believes represents the best achievement in directing.

Excellence in Cinematography

Awarded by the jury to the

documentary film which has the most outstanding cinematography.

Freedom of Expression Prize
The Freedom of Expression Prize is designed to honor and recognise courage and cinematic excellence among documentary films addressing political and human rights issues worldwide. Any documentary, national or international, screening at the festival is eligible for the award.

World Cinema Juries
Two separate juries preside over the World Cinema Competition; one focused on films in the dramatic category, the other on the documentaries. A Jury Prize is awarded by each World Cinema jury to the best film in their respective categories.

Short Film Jury
The Short Film Jury has responsibility for bestowing festival awards to the short films playing at the festival. The jury makes the following presentations:

Jury Prize in Short Filmmaking
Awarded to one of the American short films playing at the festival that exemplifies outstanding vision and creativity.

International Jury Prize in Short Filmmaking
Presented to one of the International short films playing at the festival that exemplifies outstanding vision and creativity.

Special Jury Prizes
As well as the regular awards, the dramatic, documentary, World Cinema, and short film juries all have the power to present Special Jury Prizes or Honourable Mentions in cases where they feel that a film deserves to be singled out for recognition.

Other Festival Awards
In addition to the standard and special awards handed out by the respective juries to films in the Independent Feature Film Competition and other programs at the festival, a number of additional awards are presented at the close of the event.

Audience Award
Now one of the most coveted awards of the festival, the Audience Award is presented to the film from either the Independent Feature Film Competition or American Spectrum programs which audiences have liked the most, as voted by public ballot. Separate awards go to dramatic and documentary films.

World Cinema Audience Award
As with the Audience Award for competition and American Spectrum films, the World Cinema Audience Award recognises two films — an international dramatic and a documentary feature — that audiences have voted as their favourites of the festival.

Alfred P. Sloan Prize
Provided by the Alfred P. Sloan Foundation, this prize is presented to the writer and director of an outstanding dramatic feature film focusing on science or technology as a theme, or depicting a scientist, engineer, or mathematician as a major character. Introduced at the 2003 festival, the award aims to increase the profile of independent films focusing on science and

technology. The Alfred P. Sloan Foundation and the Sundance Institute appoint a special jury to bestow the award, and the winning film receives a cash prize, split equally between the writer and director.

Sundance/NHK International Filmmakers Award

Established in 1996 by the Japan Broadcasting Corporation (NHK) in collaboration with the Sundance Institute, this award honours and supports new and independent filmmaking voices from four different regions: the United States, Europe, Latin America, and Japan. A specially appointed jury selects one winning screenplay from each region, based on the strength of the script and the filmmakers' previous work. Each award winner receives a cash prize and a commitment from NHK to purchase the Japanese broadcast rights for the finished film. The final four scripts also receive support from the Sundance Institute to help develop and finance them and distribute the final films. The winner from Latin America receives additional assistance from a group of Spanish broadcasters through a further cash prize and a pre-buy of the Spanish rights.

attending

One of the beauties of the Sundance Film Festival is that it's open to everyone. It doesn't matter whether you are a studio boss or a film fan; you pretty much have the same chance of seeing films as anyone else. No compulsory registration or accreditation is required; if you want to see any films, access official venues, or attend festival events, all you have to do is purchase either a ticket (individual or package) or a festival pass.

Pre-Registration

To cope with the explosive growth in the popularity of the festival, over the years Sundance has experimented with a range of ticket packages and festival pass types, and methods of obtaining them. The current pre-registration system was put in place for the 2005 festival as a way of decreasing wait times and generally providing a better customer experience for festivalgoers. Pre-registration works as follows:

• In early October, the Sundance Web site opens its proverbial doors for prospective Sundancers to pre-register for individual tickets, ticket packages, or festival passes. Pre-registration entails a small, non-refundable reservation fee and doors close at the end of October.

• In the first week of November, all pre-registrants receive an email containing a date, time, and information on how to purchase their individual tickets, package, or pass. Purchase dates and times are allocated randomly, so there is no advantage in pre-registering early.

• On your allocated purchase date, at your allocated time, you can buy your tickets, package, or pass, either over the phone or via a special password-protected area of the festival web site. Purchasing online is generally the preferable option as telephone purchases are subject to an additional administration fee.

As all tickets, packages, and passes are subject to availability, pre-registration does not guarantee you will get a package or pass you are interested in, however it does allow you to avoid the rush by having a *guaranteed time* to make your purchase. It's worth noting that availability for individual tickets, packages, and passes is generally better during the second half of the festival.

The introduction of any new system is bound to bring with it a little confusion and some minor teething problems. To help alleviate this, the festival has put together an extremely useful Pre-Registration FAQ which can be found at www.sundance.org.

Individual Tickets

If you pre-registered tickets to individual screenings, your randomly allocated purchase date will fall sometime during the second week of January. Based on availability, you will be able to purchase up to 20 tickets for screenings and panel events.

Once the regular festival box office opens (usually the week before the festival starts), you can also purchase tickets either by calling the festival ticket line between 10am and 6pm, buying online at www.sundance.org, or simply showing up in person at one of the box offices:

Park City
Gateway Center
136 Heber Avenue

Salt Lake City
Trolley Square, second level
700 East 500 South

The box offices are open from 10am–7pm leading up to the festival (noon–5pm on Sundays), and 8am–7pm during the event. Tickets are $10.00 each and can be purchased by cash or credit card. Tickets are also available at the Sundance Village and in Ogden.

Bear in mind that the box office opens after pre-registrants have purchased their tickets and fulfilled their ticket packages. Expect availability to be extremely limited, particularly for highly-anticipated films or events.

Ticket Packages

If you are planning to attend more than a handful of screenings, you should consider purchasing a multi-ticket package. This will make your festival visit simpler and save you money at the same time. There are two packages on offer, named for simplicity, "Ticket Package A" and "Ticket Package B". Package A is valid for the first half of the festival; Package B for the second.

Both ticket packages provide you with a total of 20 tickets, which can be used for regular screenings, Premieres, and/or panel discussions. There is a maximum of four tickets per package-holder for any given screening or event. Package A includes the option of attending the Opening Night Reception, and Package B includes the Awards Night Party.

If you pre-register for a ticket package, your randomly-allocated purchase date and time will fall during the second week of November. At this point, you simply select the flavour of package you want, but don't specify any screenings or events (since the schedule hasn't been announced yet).

In mid-December, the screening schedule is posted on the Sundance Web site, and shortly after the festival film guide is sent to ticket-package registrants. Registrants are also sent information (usually slightly ahead of the film guide) on how to select the screenings and panels for their packages. Each package holder is allocated a specific date and time in early January to order tickets, either by visiting the Web site or calling the festival box office. Tickets are then held at the registration centre at Festival HQ in Park City (but can also be mailed out ahead of time for an additional fee).

One of the key advantages of purchasing a ticket package is that you get to select your screenings a couple of weeks before general ticket sales begin. It is therefore less of a scramble to get a seat for the films you want to see. With that in mind, it's important not to miss your allocated ticket-selection time. If you postpone filling your package until after general sales begin, many screenings will already be sold out.

If, for some reason, you are a package holder who ends up not choosing all your events before the festival, you will receive vouchers for the remaining package components. These can be exchanged for tickets (subject to availability, of course) at any festival box office, or a particular

screening venue, at least one hour before the event's scheduled start time. Vouchers may also be exchanged for wait-list tickets at the screening venue (see Screenings for more information). Ticket-package vouchers are non-refundable, cannot be used in place of a ticket for a screening, and are not transferable to another person.

The price of a ticket package is in the region of $650; however there is also a handling fee of around $20 and an additional administration fee if you choose to fulfil your package over the phone. There is a limit of one package or pass per time period, and two packages/passes per person. All ticket packages include credentials for admission to Sundance House, Filmmaker Lodge, the Digital Center, and daytime admission to Music Café. Admission to these venues is only valid during the package's designated time period.

Festival Passes
The festival also offers several passes for those who want more streamlined access to the event or simply want to put off choosing which films to see. Festival passes allow you to casually stride into a screening or panel discussion while the masses huddle out in the cold, waiting to see if they can get a ticket. Well, it's almost that easy. In reality, to guarantee entry to an event, you must be at the venue at least 15 minutes before the scheduled start time, probably earlier for highly anticipated screenings.

As with ticket packages, if you pre-registered for a festival pass your randomly-allocated purchase date and time will be during the second week of November. All passes are subject to availability and the types of passes on offer (and their prices) tend to vary a little from year to year so check the festival Web site (www.sundance.org) ahead of the next festival to confirm which passes will be available.

Awards Weekend Pass
If you're planning to drop in to Park City for the last weekend of the festival, the Awards Weekend Pass is for you. It provides access to all films screening on the last Saturday and Sunday of the festival. The award-winning films are screened on the Saturday and Sunday nights. In addition to the screenings, the pass admits you to the Awards Party on Saturday night at the Park City Racquet Club, where the ceremony can be viewed on-screen via a live feed. It is not necessary to obtain tickets for screenings or the Awards Party; simply show up at least 15 minutes before the scheduled start time (earlier for the Awards Party or highly anticipated screenings). An Awards Weekend Pass costs around $200.

Adrenaline Pass
For the hardcore Sundancer, the Adrenaline Pass provides access to all screenings before 10am and after 10pm for the duration of the festival. All of the films in the Independent Feature Film Competition screen at least once during these times, and the festival schedule allows you the possibility of attending one film in the morning and two films each evening. With an Adrenaline Pass, you don't need to obtain tickets for a screening; simply show up at least 15 minutes before the scheduled start time (earlier for highly anticipated screenings). An Adrenaline Pass also admits you to the Awards Night party on the last Saturday of the festival (RSVP required). To get your mitts on this pass, you'll have to part with around $350.

Eccles Theater Pass
As with the ticket packages, there are two varieties of Eccles Theater Priority Pass: "A" covering the first half of the festival, and "B" covering the second. Eccles Theater Priority Passes provide access to screenings in the Independent Feature Film Competition and Premieres program which take place in the Eccles Theater. All films in both programs screen at the Eccles at least once during the festival. Tickets for screenings aren't required; you simply show up at least 15 minutes before the scheduled start time (earlier for highly anticipated screenings). An Eccles Theater Pass costs around $1,500.

Express Pass
Possibly the daddy of Sundance credentials, Express Passes also come in A and B flavours. Although they may be on the expensive side, Express Passes provide ultimate flexibility in attending screenings and events. With this pass, you can attend virtually any screening at any venue during the valid time period. The pass also provides entry to panel discussions during the validity dates. To secure an Express Pass, you will need to donate around $2,500 to the cause.

Similarly to the ticket packages, there is a limit of one package or pass per time period, and two packages/passes per person. In addition to screening access, all passes include credentials for admission to Sundance House, Filmmaker Lodge, the Digital Center, and daytime admission to the Music Café. Admission to these venues is only valid during the package's designated time period. All "A" passes also include the Opening Night Reception following the Premiere screening; all "B" passes include the Awards Night party on the last Saturday of the festival. RSVPs are essential for both events.

Additional Information

Questions regarding packages and passes can be directed to Festival Customer Service via email to festival registration@sundance.org.

If, for some reason, you need to cancel your ticket package or pass, you must make a request in writing to the Sundance Registration Office. A 20 percent handling fee is levied on cancellations, and all requests must be received by the end of the second week of December (check the exact date on the festival Web site). Refunds are not given after this time.

Passes and ticket packages can be picked up from the registration centre in Festival HQ from the first day of the festival, and throughout the event. Alternatively, for a fee of around $25 you can have your package or pass express delivered ahead of the festival and skip the registration queues.

Film Industry Professionals

Even in the early days of the Utah/US Film Festival, Sundance was always a popular event for film industry professionals. Indeed, one of the core goals for the event was to attract more filmmakers to Utah so that the state economy could benefit from the large direct investment when a major film is shot.

As the festival matured, distribution companies, large and small, began to make the trek to Park City, hoping to bag an undiscovered indie gem that would net them millions at the worldwide box office. However, the explosion of interest the festival witnessed during the 1990s also attracted professionals from many other sectors of the industry, keen to take advantage of the excellent networking opportunities, have a look at the best that the independent film world had to offer, and in some cases, simply take a ski holiday they could write off as a business trip.

These days, Sundance is a major event on the industry calendar, not only for sales agents and acquisition executives, but also for a host of other people in the industry. Approximately 30 percent of attendees have some form of industry affiliation. In recent years, Sundance has been busily expanding the range of services offered to film industry professionals, with their efforts culminating in the creation of the Sundance Industry Office.

The Sundance Industry Office is an information resource for industry attendees and is the hub of official industry-related activity at the festival.

Services offered by the new industry office include priority pass/package selection, a new industry office pass, a video library for festival films, and an online directory containing contact information and profiles for festival filmmakers and accredited industry participants.

For more information, email the Sundance Industry Office - sio@sundance.org - or visit the festival Web site at www.sundance.org.

The business side of the festival is explored in more detail in part three of this book, The Biz.

Press Accreditation

Sundance is a major media event on the film calendar, and each year the festival welcomes more than 800 members of the national and international press. There are four different flavours of press accreditation, and these are doled out based on the profile of the individual and/or organisation, the type of media represented, and the level of access required.

Press accreditation is managed by the Festival Press Office and is available to approved members of print, audiovisual, and online press. The press office begins accepting requests for accreditation in September each year (and it's worth noting that the allocation of a specific type of press badge is at the sole discretion of the press office).

If you are a new applicant for press credentials, you must submit the following items to support your application:

• a completed application form;

• a passport-sized photograph;

• an example of your publication or program (print media — a copy of your publication; online media — the URL for your site; television/radio — a recording of your show);

• a letter from your editor or producer on company letterhead, assigning you to cover the festival (this should include a description of the media outlet);

• information on the areas of the festival you intend to cover;

• a statement of intent to broadcast or publish coverage of the festival;

• a copy of an article or program (depending on your media type) written/made by you that focuses on film, a film festival, or entertainment in general.

Requests for press accreditation should be directed to:

Sundance Institute
Attn: Press Office
307 West 200 South
Suite 5002
Salt Lake City, UT 84101
Tel. 801-328-3456
Fax. 801-575-5175
press@sundance.org

The deadline for press accreditation requests is usually mid-November each year, and applicants are normally notified of the status of their request within a couple of weeks.

Volunteering

Can't afford a festival package or pass? Not interested in messing around with single tickets? Don't qualify as a member of the press? Never fear, you still have a chance of attending the festival... by volunteering to help out.

An event on the scale of the Sundance Film Festival requires the coordinated efforts of a huge number of people, far more than the festival budget can realistically cover. Sundance gets around this labour problem by offering eager beavers (you need to be fairly eager because some of the jobs involve standing outside in the cold and being nice to people for long periods of time) the chance to volunteer to help out. Each year, more than 1,100 volunteers take on duties such as venue management and staffing, merchandise sales, transportation marshalling, and customer service. Depending on the type of job and the number of hours worked, festival volunteers receive a variety of benefits, including access to festival screenings and official venues, invites to official evening parties, and a free volunteer uniform.

There are two types of volunteer positions at the Sundance Film Festival, and the requirements and benefits vary slightly between the two:

Full-Time Volunteers
Full-time volunteers must commit to a pre-assigned schedule of around 8–10 hours each day for the duration of the festival; they must also be available to attend the pre-festival training sessions. In return for this effort, full-time volunteers receive a volunteer pass that admits them to films, panel discussions, and evening parties on a space-available

basis. A percentage of full-time volunteers also receive housing for the duration of the event. At the end of the festival, Sundance may also give full-time volunteers a small cash reimbursement for travel and meal expenses.

Sign-Up Volunteers
Sign-up volunteers work both pre-festival and during the event on a flexible-hours basis. Sign-up volunteers must make their own arrangements for lodging in Park City, but in return for their services, they receive volunteer vouchers or a volunteer pass (depending on the number of hours worked) that admits them to films, panel discussions, and evening parties on a space-available basis.

Although most positions are usually offered to returning volunteers first, the festival welcomes applications from new recruits. All volunteers must be at least 21 years old and must arrange their own transportation to the festival. If you are considering applying to volunteer for Sundance, you should explore your travel and lodging options before you submit an application.

Applications can be submitted year-round through the Sundance Institute Web site (www.sundance.org, look in the Support the Institute section); however, the festival doesn't usually begin reviewing applications until October. The decision to accept and assign volunteers for the event is based on several factors, including the number of people required, the skills you have to offer, the dates you are available, and your overall enthusiasm. Volunteers accepted for the festival are notified by mid-December.

Completed volunteer applications should either be submitted online or sent to:

Sundance Institute
P.O. Box 3630
Salt Lake City
UT 84110-3630
U.S.A.

For more information on volunteering, contact the volunteer manager at the Sundance Institute at 801-328-3456 or volunteers@sundance.org.

Picking Up Your Credentials
For a smooth and painless festival experience, you should carry your festival credentials at all times. If you haven't already received it, your first mission after you arrive in Park City is picking up your badge. The place to do this depends on the type of credential you've requested:

Ticket Packages/Passes
These can be picked up from the registration centre at Festival HQ once the festival starts, or you can have them mailed out to you in early January for a fee of $25. If you ask for your package/pass to be sent, but don't receive it in time for the festival, either contact Customer Service at the Sundance Registration Office or visit the registration centre at Festival HQ in Park City starting on the first Wednesday of the event.

Press Credentials
These are available from the Festival Press Office, located at Festival HQ,

starting the day before the festival and throughout the event.

Volunteer Credentials
These are handed out during the volunteer training days before the festival.

screenings

Screenings are of course the bread and butter of any festival and also the main reason most people make the trek to Park City. With more than 200 films in the festival program, cinema lovers are never going to be strapped for choices. For the extremely dedicated, screenings kick-off at 8:30am and continue through to the fabled midnight slots. One of the great things about Sundance is that, unlike many other film festivals, all of the films are screened in different venues on different days throughout the event. This makes it considerably easier to catch all the films you want to see. However, for the truly hardcore Sundancer, getting to see all the films on your list demands meticulously planned strategy, followed by flawless execution.

Perhaps the most important component of a good Sundance strategy is getting to know the films that will screen during the festival. Whilst the film guide is a great place to start, space limitations mean that the information on each film is always fairly brief. Consequently, it's usually best to supplement this with your own research. Keep an ear to the ground by talking to other festivalgoers about things they liked, things they didn't, and, of course, things they're looking forward to. It's also a great way to make new friends, and since you're all in town for the same reason — a passion for movies — most people usually have something interesting to say.

Another good reason to take a little time to research the films is to make sure you don't get any unpleasant surprises. Most films shown at the festival are not rated, so viewer discretion is strongly advised. For those who are easily offended or plan to bring children to a screening, doing your research and getting to know the films are doubly important to ensure your festival experience is enjoyable.

So where are the best places to conduct your research? Wherever the opportunity presents itself! This can be while you're standing in line for a screening — nobody likes waiting, and striking up a conversation offers friendly relief from boredom — or perhaps in one of the official venues, such as Sundance House or the Filmmaker Lodge. Another good prospect is on the shuttle bus between venues, or indeed, while you're waiting for the bus to arrive. Actually, this is one of the best places to pick up reliable film buzz since the volunteers who staff the bus stops have the opportunity to chat with a huge number of people and are therefore in one of the best positions to know what films everyone's talking about.

Researching films before the festival is also useful, but the nature of independent filmmaking often means that there is little or no information about some films before the Sundance screenings. This doesn't mean you should give up on the idea, though. Try Web sites like the Internet Movie Database (www.imdb.com) or check the trade press, particularly publications with an independent bias such as indieWIRE (www.indiewire.com). And remember, Google is your friend (www.google.com).

Of course, even the best-laid plans can run into grief, and, given the popularity of the festival, there is always a chance that the screening you planned to attend is sold out before you can get into the theatre. For this reason, it's important to ensure your plan includes alternatives for those (hopefully rare) times when the powers that be end up foiling your attempt to see a specific film, and you're literally left out in the cold. Alternatives can be other films, but don't forget about the various panel discussions and seminars, particularly those in the Filmmaker Lodge and the Sundance Digital Center, which are often just walk-in events. And although it can be hard to contemplate when you are surrounded by all that is the Sundance Film Festival, you also shouldn't discount the value of using your newfound free time for something besides another screening. Eating is a good pastime, particularly if you've set yourself a punishing film-going schedule and haven't allowed sufficient time for refuelling, and even taking the opportunity to catch a few Zs can be most rewarding.

As far as getting into a screening goes, it's a relatively painless experience, regardless of whether you've chosen the single-ticket route, a ticket package, or a festival pass.

This is of course assuming you show up on time. Your ticket, package, or pass only guarantees entry to the screening until 15 minutes before the scheduled start time; after that the wait list is activated, and your seat will be given to someone else. Remember that the January weather in Park City can be variable, and consequently, it may end up taking longer to get to a venue than normal (particularly if you foolishly decide to drive to your screening). For pass holders, missing a screening is simply a mild annoyance since you can potentially catch the film at another venue on another day. For single-ticket or package holders, however, missing a screening can spell disaster, resulting in you missing the film entirely since all tickets are non-refundable and non-exchangeable after the screening. The moral of the story is to make sure you allow yourself plenty of time to get to your screening.

Post-Screening Q&As

Those who bolt for the door the second the credits hit the screen will lose out at Sundance. Not only is it extremely bad film-going manners to act this way at a premiere, but you will also miss out on one of the greatest things about attending a Sundance screening — the opportunity to listen to (and take part in) the post-screening question and answer (Q&A) session with the filmmakers.

In most cases, the film's director and one or more of its stars are present for the Q&A following the screening. This is your chance to pop them that question which has been burning in your mind since the close of Act II, or find out more about how the film made it to the screen. Often

the stories behind the making of a film are every bit as interesting as the films themselves (sometimes, more interesting). Don't waste this opportunity by bailing out early.

Venues

As a mining town turned ski resort, the number of venues suitable for hosting a world-class film festival in Park City has always been on the thin side. However, in true independent spirit, the festival makes do. Films showing in Park City during the festival screen at the following venues:

Eccles Theater

A dedicated arts complex attached to the Park City High School, the Eccles Center was completed in 1998 and is the newest and largest of the festival screening venues. The Eccles has 1,270 seats in the main theatre and a small press-screening area known as the Eccles Black Box. You can find the Eccles Center at 1750 Kearns Boulevard.

Egyptian Theater

Officially known as the Mary G. Steiner Egyptian Theater, Park City's first cinema was built in 1926 as a replica of the famous Warner's Egyptian Theater in Pasadena, California. Although the theatre is small (a pokey 296 seats), its distinctive interior and exterior décor has made it one of the most recognisable festival icons. The Egyptian Theater is located toward the top of Main Street (number 328).

Holiday Village Cinemas

Park City's local miniplex is commandeered during the festival and serves as a venue for both press and public shows. There are four small theatres inside, each with 150 seats. The Holiday Village Cinemas are located in the shopping center behind the Yarrow Hotel.

Park City Library Center Theater

The former high school now houses the city's public library and hosts University of Utah extension classes, but also boasts a reasonably large auditorium (468 seats). Consequently, it has become one of the main screening venues for festival films and the most notorious amongst festivalgoers for its uncomfortable seats. The Park City Library Center is located on Park Avenue about halfway between Main Street and Kearns Boulevard.

Park City Racquet Club

For 2005 (and presumably beyond), in addition to hosting the closing night awards ceremony, the racquet club will also be commandeered for transformation into the seventh Park City screening venue.

Prospector Square Theater

This 360-seat venue has become an integral part of the festival screening circuit and is located in the Prospector Square area at 2200 Sidewinder Drive (down the street from Festival HQ).

Yarrow Theater

For most of the year, the Yarrow is simply one of Park City's top hotels; however, during the festival its extensive banquet halls are transformed into mini-cinemas. A selection of festival films are screened here in the 250-seat Yarrow Theater, and the hotel is also the main press-screening venue (known as the Yarrow Press-Screening Room). The Yarrow Hotel is located on the corner of Park Avenue and Kearns Boulevard.

Outside of Park City

Although the bulk of the screenings take place in Park City, a selection of festival films are also shown in Salt Lake City, Kimball Junction, Ogden, and at the Sundance Village. Non-Park City screenings vary from year to year, but are always listed in the online film guide and festival film guide.

Finding Out What's On Where

The best place to get the lowdown on screening times and locations is the online film guide at the festival Web site (www.sundance.org). The online film guide usually goes live in the second week of December, and the printed film guide becomes available shortly after. Both the online guide and the printed film guide include a full screening schedule, indicating times, dates, and venues, and noting Premiere screenings (which are usually attended by the filmmakers and key cast members).

Day-of-Show Tickets

As a rule, all but the most obscure films are completely sold out by the time the festival begins. However, for a variety of reasons, there is a slim possibility that tickets may become available for some screenings. Where this is the case, the festival sells these as day-of-show tickets at the main box offices. Tickets are released daily at 8am for films screening that day (although tickets for early screenings are usually released the day before). All tickets must be purchased in person; there are no online or phone orders for day-of-show tickets. In the unlikely event that there are still day-of-show tickets available after the box offices close, these are sold at the individual theatres prior to the show. If you're intent on seeing a film but don't have a pass or a ticket, it's worth trying your luck. Remember that day-of-show-ticket success is inversely proportionate to the profile of the screening, and you always have a better chance at a bigger venue.

Wait-List Tickets

Even if you don't have a ticket or pass for a screening you're just burning to attend, so long as you're at the venue early enough, there's a good chance you can get in via the wait-list ticket system. About an hour before the scheduled start time, numbered wait-list cards are handed out at the screening venue on a first-come, first-served basis (with up to two cards per person).

Approximately 30 minutes before the start time, festival staff begin selling wait-list tickets to card holders in the order of the number on their card. Wait-list tickets are a flat $10 each and can only be paid for in cash. Finally, 15 minutes before the screening commences, the venue management surveys the theatre, and wait-list ticket holders are admitted, based on the number of seats available, until the venue is full (and again, in order of card number). Refunds are then issued to anyone who purchased a wait-list ticket, but is unable to get into the screening.

The wait list represents the best chance of seeing a film which you don't have a ticket or valid pass for; however, the most important words to remember are *get there early*. Wait-list cards may be handed out an hour before the show, but the line for them forms considerably earlier. As with day-of-show tickets, your chance of success on the wait list is inversely proportionate to the profile of the screening — the lower the profile, the more chance you have of getting in — and the bigger the venue, the better your chances of wait-list success. Since most venues operate multiple lines for different types of patrons, be sure you are standing in the correct line for wait-list tickets.

TBAs

If you look through the schedule of films in the film guide, you may notice an occasional slot noted as TBA. This stands for "To Be Announced" and is a place holder in the schedule which allows festival programmers to add additional screenings of popular films once the festival begins. Information on TBAs is available at each of the theatres and festival box offices, as well as the festival newsletter, which debuted in 2004.

Ticket Exchange

Over the past few years, the massive growth in the number of screenings (and therefore tickets) has led to a rather ugly problem: people getting tickets for films and not showing up. This not only causes management nightmares at the screening venues, but also robs other festivalgoers of a chance to see the film. In an effort to alleviate the problem, Sundance has implemented a ticket-exchange system. Ticket exchange now allows you to swap your unwanted tickets for another screening (subject to availability, of course). For $2 per ticket, you may exchange your tickets 24 hours before the printed screening time at the main box offices. If your screening is after 7pm, you must exchange your tickets earlier on the day before.

Collecting Tickets (Will Call)

Festivalgoers who select Will Call when buying tickets must pick them up at the Park City or Salt Lake City main box offices (based on which location you choose at the time of purchase) between 8am and 7pm. Will Call is no longer available at the individual theatre box offices. Tickets for screenings after 7pm must be picked up during regular box-office hours. Package and pass holders who select Will Call must pick up passes and packages at the registration centre at Festival HQ in Park City, open from 8am to 6pm. Festivalgoers with first screenings in Ogden or at the Sundance Village need to pick up their tickets for that screening only at the theatre box office.

Express Delivery

Sundance now offers festivalgoers the opportunity to have their tickets and credentials sent out prior to the start of the event. For $25, you can have them mailed by express delivery in early January.

Press Screenings

If you're attending the festival as an accredited member of the media, your press credentials will get you into most press screenings of festival films. There are three main press-screening venues at Sundance:

Yarrow Press-Screening Room (inside the Yarrow Hotel)

Eccles Black Box Press-Screening Room (at the Eccles Center)

Holiday Village Cinemas (one of the screens is usually requisitioned for press screenings during the day)

The press-screening venues are all reasonably small, and with 800-strong press corps in town, it's important to get there early for any of the highly anticipated films. On arrival, you should register with the festival staff at the door. Film publicists usually hand out production notes and press kits, either when you get there, or once you're inside the screening room.

The schedule for the press screenings is coordinated by the Festival Press Office and is a constantly evolving beast. A trip to the press office at Festival HQ first thing in the morning should therefore become part of any journalist's daily routine.

parties and hanging out

All film festivals are as much about the social aspects of bringing together a diverse group of people who share a single thing in common — a love of film — as they are about the films themselves. Socialising (and networking) is an essential part of every festival experience, manifesting itself through meeting people in casual hangouts and, of course, attending parties. And as far as Sundance goes, there is a whole host of ways to kick back, party hard, meet new friends, or just hang out with old ones.

Official Evening Parties

Many big film festivals are legendary for their parties (sometimes more than for their films); however, one of the most disappointing things at some festivals is the fact that these legendary parties are often entirely invitation only and therefore closed to most festivalgoers. A wonderfully refreshing thing about Sundance is that a series of evening parties are held throughout the festival, allowing festivalgoers to socialise with filmmakers, sponsors, and the press at several spectacular locations in and around the town.

The official party schedule kicks off on opening night in Park City with the bottom of Main Street exorcised of cars and the resulting void filled with partygoers enjoying a mix of live music, DJs, and street performances. As the evening matures, the Sundancing moves up Main Street to Harry O's nightclub and the Music Café. The opening-night street party is open to all festivalgoers.

To keep the celebratory spirit rolling throughout the event, Sundance and festival sponsors host a slate of official evening parties at regular intervals. The dates and locations of these parties vary from festival to festival, so you need to check the film guide or Web site for this year's events. Sponsors cover a large chunk of the catering budget for most of these events (meaning drinks and finger food are included), but most parties move to a cash bar later on. Aside from the opening night celebration on Main Street, entry to virtually all official evening parties requires an appropriate ticket.

Remember, unless you are famous, there's no such thing as "fashionably late" in Park City. Party space is limited and sponsored booze finite, so it's important to make sure you arrive on time if you a) want to get in, and b) don't want to spend a fortune on drinks.

Unofficial Parties

Whilst the official parties are a breath of fresh air for their egalitarian approach, the most notorious Sundance parties are those thrown by publicists for films in the festival program, by visiting film companies, and by the alternative festivals (such as Slamdance). Historically, unofficial parties were less-organised affairs, usually with their main claim to fame being an attempt to set a new world record for how many people could be squeezed into one condo. These days, the festival profile and the ever-increasing industry attendance have resulted in more organised affairs, with fancy locations, corporate sponsors, private guest lists, and heavy security. This can make finding out about a party, let alone attending it, quite a challenge.

So how do you get to rub shoulders with the Park City in-crowd? Simple. You either work your contact network to find out who's throwing a bash and see if you can orchestrate an invite; or you make new friends in Park City and discretely pump them for information and, more importantly, ways of getting on the guest list. Failing that, you can try contacting the event organisers directly, then, using your boundless wit and creativity, explain why you should be allowed to come to their shindig. Party crashing is of course an art form unto itself and a bit like a career in filmmaking: There is no single route in, but if you are dedicated, talented, lucky, and smart, you'll probably find a way.

Regardless of how you manage to secure an invite, the advice about not being "fashionably late" is even more important for unofficial events. An oft-quoted line at an affair a few years ago sums up this situation perfectly: A large crowd of revellers was waiting outside a crowded Deer Valley condo party one night. Increasingly frustrated, a member of the door security team was heard to shout, "The party is full. You're not getting in unless you're famous...and I don't recognise any of you!"

Once You're In

A lot of how you approach a party once you're inside depends on whether you are visiting Sundance for business or pleasure. If you're just in town to see some movies, you can simply kick back and enjoy the atmosphere and refreshments. However, if you're doing Sundance with a business agenda, most parties involve walking that fine line between having a good time and keeping on top of your work objectives.

Parties offer a great opportunity to meet people in a relaxed setting, and indeed, people whom you otherwise might find difficult to see. It's therefore important that you spend your party time being friendly and outgoing. Don't simply hang out in a big group with your mates. Be bold and introduce yourself to people whenever the opportunity arises.

It's also a good idea to try and take most people you meet seriously. Inevitably, you will meet some people who you feel are just wasting space on this planet, but you never know how important they may become (now or in the future). Consequently, you should be polite, steer clear of conversation that provokes strong reaction (i.e., religion, politics, or how crappy the film you saw today was), and be careful with jokes since not everyone may have the same great sense of humour as you. Finally, remember to take it easy on the alcohol (particularly given the added effects of altitude) since you want to stay sharp and coherent in case you meet anyone important.

Daytime Hanging Out

There will be times when you're not at a screening or participating in any of Park City's other recreational activities when simply kicking back is just what the doctor ordered (particularly if your screening and party schedule has been rather intense). Fortunately, your hangout options are plentiful.

The official venues, particularly Sundance House, the Filmmaker Lodge, the Sundance Digital Center, and the Music Café, are designed for daytime hanging out. All offer some form of café-style environment where you can sit down for a bit, meet with people, grab a drink or bite to eat, or just kick back and relax.

Outside of the official venues, the options really depend on what sort of mood you're in. For those in search of coffee, Bad Ass Coffee at 651 Park Avenue or Starbucks (corner of Park Avenue and Iron Horse Drive) can fulfil all your caffeine needs. If you're lusting after more of a bar scene, head for one of the many establishments along Main Street. Try The Claimjumper (number 573), O'Shucks Bar & Grill (number 427), J.B. Mulligan's Irish Pub (number 804), or The Phat Tire Saloon if you're a smoker in need of an indoor puff. Off Main Street, try Renee's at 136 Heber Avenue, where you can relax on large red couches sipping a cup of coffee, glass of wine, or even a martini if you so desire.

After Dark

Once the sun sets over the Wasatch Mountains, your options for a good night out are almost limitless in Park City. The high density of nightspots in the town has resulted in stiff competition, so most venues try their utmost to put on a good night for patrons. And what's more, the free festival and city busses mean that a big night out doesn't come with the usual "how am I going to get home?" worries.

A local favourite is Mother Urban's at 625 Main Street on the corner of Heber Avenue. Located in the town's former red-light district and named after a 200-pound madam who walked on a peg leg during Park City's mining days, this cellar bar hosts a range of live music performances on the weekends and is more laid back earlier in the week. If a casual sports bar is more your thing, upstairs at Burgies at 570 Main Street will be just your cup of tea. The environment is extremely casual, the food fast and plentiful, and there's a great balcony where you can watch the traffic as it passes below on Main Street (and we're not really talking cars here). Of course, that is if you don't mind the cold and the mad puffers.

If the night finds you in the mood for DJs and dancing, the Sundance Music Café at 268 Main Street is a good place to get your blood pumping. There's also Harry O's at 427 Main Street, which is the largest venue in town and hosts a wide variety of DJs and live music acts well into the wee hours.

the
biz

"For us, the most important aspect of Sundance is launching our films. It's really the only place other than the Cannes Film Festival — in some ways it's better — where you have this number of critics in one spot at one time."

Michael Barker
Co-president, Sony Pictures Classics

"'Sundance' is actually an old Indian word that means 'publicity'; few people know that."

Eric Stoltz
Actor

the biz

Ever since the very first Utah/US Film Festival in 1978, there has been a business agenda of some kind at the festival. Back then the main goal was to attract more Hollywood filmmakers to Utah in the hope of persuading them to shoot their films in the state and thereby boost the local economy. These days, as the Sundance Film Festival, the event continues to have a business agenda, although it has quite a different complexion.

Although historically there has been no official apparatus to support it, Sundance has emerged as one of the key film-industry events of the year, particularly for anyone involved in sales and acquisitions. Indeed, the purchasing antics of distributors in Park City during recent years have generated almost as many column inches as the festival films. But even though sales and acquisitions get the lion's share of attention, many industry people also drop in to Park City for other reasons. According to the official statistics, around 30 percent of people who register with the festival for a ticket package or pass say they have some type of industry affiliation. However, the true number of industry people in town during the festival is probably somewhat higher than this because many people who come to Park City for business don't actually sign up for packages or passes.

Aside from the press, the largest single contingent of industry people in Park City during the festival is of course those who work in sales and acquisitions or in areas which directly support sales (i.e., publicity). Typically, industry people who are not involved in these areas are filmmakers (predominantly producers, directors, and writers), equipment vendors, facility providers, and of course agents. For these people, the business side of the festival is mainly about meetings and networking, although some filmmakers may of course also be involved in selling their films.

Business at Sundance is, for the most part, focused on the U.S. industry and these days leans more toward a place where "Indiewood" meets Hollywood than anything else. But in recent years, the overseas profile of the festival has been steadily growing, and this has resulted in an increasing number of foreign companies becoming involved in the event; although, to date, these people have mainly been buyers looking to pick up home territory rights to festival films, or international sales agents representing movies in the World Cinema programs. Increasingly, Sundance is becoming more important as a launch pad for English-language films, so activity from companies in countries like Australia, Canada, Ireland, New Zealand, and the U.K. will probably increase as time goes by.

business at sundance

On the whole, business at Sundance is a pretty informal affair. Sales agents, publicists, acquisitions executives, and journalists tend to be insanely busy, but for the remainder of attendees, the festival almost has the feel of a working holiday. However, this casual nature can be both a benefit and a hindrance for those trying to do business in Park City. On the plus side, everyone is considerably more laid back and approachable than they are at home; on the downside, the lack of a formalised market structure means that it can be much harder to find the people you need to see than at a comparable event.

Business at Sundance tends to fall into three main areas, and if you're heading to Park City with a work agenda, it's important to understand how each of these areas operates.

Sales and Acquisitions

Ever since *sex, lies and videotape* bowed in 1989, a huge amount of media hype has surrounded the acquisitions activity at the festival. This has helped create and perpetuate a myth that Sundance is some kind of acquisitions bonanza, where any independent filmmaker can walk in with their self-financed feature and walk out with a $5-million deal from Harvey Weinstein.

The reality is, of course, rather different. Whilst it's true that many exceptional deals were made at the festival during the 1990s when the independent film movement was on its meteoric rise, these were the exception rather than the rule. For every Clerks, *El Mariachi*, Brothers McMullen, or The Blair Witch Project, there are at least 10 other films that never saw any acquisitions money at the festival, and sometimes no money at all. Acquisitions activity at Sundance in the new millennium has been sobered by the kind of perspective that can only be provided by the passage of time and a string of disappointing box-office figures for over-hyped films. As a result, distributors are prepared to take far fewer risks than they were a couple of years ago, and it has become even harder for films without some kind of name attached to make a big acquisitions splash in Park City.

That said, a fair amount of acquisitions activity does still go on at Sundance. As the first major festival of the year, Sundance provides an opportunity for an early look many films, particularly the Premieres, those in the Independent Feature Film Competition, and many foreign films in World Cinema. Most of the deals are usually made by the specialty divisions of the major and mini-major studios, such as Miramax, Fine Line, or Fox Searchlight, and involve picking up the worldwide or major-territory rights to buzz films. Acquisitions activity normally focuses primarily on Premieres and features in the Independent Feature Film Competition and American Spectrum program; however, films in World Cinema often get attention, either for their U.S. rights or wider rights, if they're still available.

Sundance still generates a degree of caution in foreign buyers, and consequently, overseas sales currently only account for a very small part of the overall sales activity. This is partly due to a lingering perception that Sundance is mainly an American festival, but also because historically, buying and selling in Park City has been quite difficult due to the lack of any formalised structure. The situation has also not been helped by a slump in revenues from the sale of American independent films overseas.

However, in the face of all this, activity from foreign buyers at Sundance is on the increase. With the American Film Market (AFM) moving from February to November in 2004 and increased efforts from the Festival itself to simplify the buying and selling process, a small, but growing, number of foreign buyers now make the trek to Park City to survey the landscape for the coming year and occasionally pick up rights for their local territories (either directly or by working with the U.S. distributor who holds the worldwide rights). International television buyers also increasingly focus on the competition and World Cinema documentary films as a source of interesting factual programming for their networks.

Meetings and Networking

The passage of time has proved Sydney Pollack was bang on the money when he suggested the festival move to Park City. Today, Hollywood does indeed "beat the door down to attend," but so, too, do a range of filmmakers and professionals from all sectors of the industry.

For those not in sales and acquisitions, Sundance is about seeing movies, catching up with friends, and generally increasing one's contact network. Meetings tend to be less formal than at home — usually taking place over a meal or in a condo which has been commandeered by a company for the duration of the event — and more focused on discussion than action. Meetings at Sundance are often the primer or first step in a larger process, with the real business transacted once everyone gets back home.

Networking also takes up a big chunk of most people's Sundance business agenda, and it's really about making new contacts that may be useful in the future. Of course, some networking is also about generating new business opportunities, particularly for agents or equipment/service vendors, but even that can be useful. Although it's common for most networking to take place after hours — either at one of the parties (official or not) or in the multitude of bars and restaurants that riddle the town — some socialising also goes on during the day at venues such as Sundance House, the Filmmaker Lodge, or the Digital Center.

Development and Financing

The number of films in the Sundance program is now very large, and once you add all the other films screening in the alternative festivals, there are suddenly a hell of a lot of films for the industry to digest in 10 days. As you can imagine, this tends to force the focus onto completed films, so it's rare to see much in the way of development or financing done at Sundance. Certainly meetings may take place between filmmakers and sales agents or acquisitions executives regarding upcoming projects, but most of the serious talking (and all of the deal making) is normally completed away from the festival. This is particularly true when the project isn't "packaged" (i.e., doesn't have one or more names attached) or doesn't have part of its financing in place.

preparing for sundance

If you decide to head to Sundance with a business agenda, it's essential to prepare your game plan well ahead of time. You need to have a clear idea about why you are attending and what you want to achieve. Without it, you run the risk of wasting your time in Park City and possibly quite a bit of money in the process. But perhaps the biggest risk of heading to Sundance sans plan is the possibility of inadvertently messing people around. For a global industry, the film business is very insular. People hold grudges, and if you mess somebody around, it may be much harder to make things happen in the future.

The first part of your Sundance preparation should therefore involve thinking about why you actually want to go to the festival in the first place. Are you going to see films, meet people, sell your movie, or perhaps all three? Each of these reasons alone requires comprehensive planning, and if you're considering all of them, extensive preparation is even more important.

Seeing Films
Although seeing films may not be the main focus of a business agenda per say, it's an important consideration if you are heading to town for anything other than a bit of R&R. Once you

are in Park City, surrounded by all that is Sundance, you will almost definitely be tempted to catch a couple of movies.

Clearly the initial concern is how you're going to be able to get into the screenings, so the first step of your planning involves securing yourself tickets or a festival credential. Individual tickets and ticket packages of course lock you into specific screenings, so if you choose one of these routes for film watching, you need to build each screening slot into your overall schedule. If you get a pass, you have more flexibility in terms of which screenings you attend, but it's more than likely that, if you spend big for a pass, you'll probably want to get your money's worth by seeing as many films as possible.

For those who are heading to the festival with a slate of business objectives, it's really important to make sure that attending screenings is an activity built into your overall schedule, not just a last-minute decision. Once you take into account the waiting time, the possibility of the screening starting late, watching the film itself, and finally the post-show Q&A, attending movies can take big chunks out of your day. During much of this time, your mobile phone will be off (well, it should be if you have any consideration for other filmgoers), and being out of contact for so long can make doing business that much more difficult. In a nutshell, it's essential to make sure you think about how going to films impacts your business agenda.

Meeting People
Going to Sundance to meet people

is an excellent way to expand your contact network and also see people from other cities who normally have a plane ticket between you and their offices. Meeting people in Park City usually happens in one of two ways: Either you arrange a meeting with someone prior to arriving in town (or perhaps while you're there), or you bump into someone along the way and, for whatever reason, you hit it off.

A big part of your preparation for Sundance should involve taking the time to set up meetings before you get to Park City. Many people who are working at Sundance are extremely busy, so not only does arranging meetings before you get there help with your own planning, but having it in someone's diary ahead of the festival dramatically increases the chance the meeting will actually happen. In saying that, you should only prearrange meetings with someone if you actually have a reason to meet. Discussing projects, pitching ideas, and talking finance are all good reasons to meet. Meetings to introduce yourself or find out more about what someone does should be barroom or party conversations, not formal meetings.

The second way of meeting people is obviously a little more serendipitous: You just have to be in the right place at the right time. You can boost your chances of meeting appropriate kinds of people by doing things like hanging out at official venues such as Sundance House, the Filmmaker Lodge, or the Digital Center. Networking and meeting people is of course also a major part of attending parties (both official and not), and

you also shouldn't discount the value of chatting with people when you're standing in line for anything from a coffee to a screening.

Whilst it's difficult to prepare specifically for these types of meetings, you can help your chances by building some hangout time into your Sundance schedule and picking venues where the type of people you want to meet are likely to congregate.

Selling Films
Of all the business activities undertaken at Sundance, selling films is by far the hardest and most intense. To achieve success in this area, your preparation needs to be meticulous, your execution flawless, and your enthusiasm boundless (with a good deal of luck thrown in on top). The first step of your preparation for selling a film at Sundance should be to seek professional representation. This means getting a sales agent onboard and, if your budget can stretch to it, a publicist as well.

There are several reasons why having at least a sales agent for your film is absolutely essential. Firstly, a reputable sales agent knows the marketplace and has the necessary contacts to get the right people into your screening. Without these contacts, you are fighting an uphill battle to get distributors to see your film. Secondly, when it comes to making a deal, having the negotiations done by a third party who's familiar with the shape of distribution agreements and is as keen as you are to sell the film (since their commission depends on it) is essential to ensure you get the best possible terms. Finally, if you've approached a large number of sales agents and they've all decided to pass, there is a good chance that your film just isn't up to scratch. As harsh as that sounds, finding out your film has little or no commercial value before you blow a load of your own money on a trip to Park City is certainly better than coming home empty-handed with a lighter wallet.

So how do you find a sales agent? The strategy used by most independent filmmakers who are starting out usually involves getting your hands on a "product guide" from one of the big international markets, such as Cannes, MIFED, or AFM. Product guides are produced by the markets themselves and also by trade magazines like *Variety* and *Screen International* (who sometimes refer to them as market "previews"). These guides are, in effect, directories of buyers and sellers who are attending each market. Although no such guide exists for Sundance, most companies who attend the big markets will also be in Park City for the festival. Pick up a copy of these guides by contacting the markets or trade magazines directly (see Appendix II for details) or canvass your contact network to see if anyone has a copy you can borrow. Even if you can only lay your hands on last year's edition, that will do fine. The major players don't change that often, so you shouldn't be overly concerned if you can't obtain a product guide for the most recent event.

Once you have your guide, devour every detail, searching for sales agents who seem to be selling films similar to your own. It's important to pick the right type of sales agent

since there's no point taking your quirky Gen-X comedy to a company that specialises in period drama. Using the details in the guide, compile your hit list and start approaching these people and companies to see if they're interested in taking on your film. You'll get plenty of rejections, but that's part of the game. You just have to keep plugging away. It's always best to start the process as far ahead of the festival as you possibly can because, ideally, you want to involve your sales agent (and publicist) in the Sundance submission process.

After you have assembled your professional team of a sales agent and hopefully a publicist, the next step is to try and get your film into the festival. Films that screen in one of the official Sundance programs are able to garner much more press (and therefore acquisitions) attention than those being shown independently. If your film isn't selected for Sundance, however, a fallback is one of the alternative festivals that run in Park City at the same time. Whilst these attract significantly less sales attention than being in the Sundance program, the fact that they are organised and publicised events means that your film has at least some chance of being noticed.

Regardless of whether you are accepted into Sundance or one of the alternative festivals, your sales agent and publicist will be able to work with you to complete your sales strategy and ensure that you're fully prepared before you arrive in Park City. Don't waste your time with trailers of clips of your film. If you are going to get people interested in your movie, it's the finished product you should be showing. If people are too busy to watch the entire film in Park City (which is quite likely), you should arrange a full screening for another time. Trailers are a tool used by distributors to market films to the general public. Most distributors know that it's very easy to misrepresent a film with a trailer, so they would rather see the whole thing.

Projects in Development
With the industry focused on completed films, pushing your project in development in Park City probably doesn't represent a worthwhile investment of your time or money. It is better to consider other events in less-expensive surroundings which have a more formalised market structure in place.

If you are hell-bent on pitching your project in Park City, the major piece of advice is keep it brief. Most of the people you want to talk to are extremely busy, and if you do manage to get someone's attention, you need to make the best use of it. Don't bother bringing clips or trailers you've put together for a film that isn't made yet — these often do more harm than good. Also don't bring scripts for people in Park City because no one has time to read them there, nor wants the excess baggage on the way home. Your script will be the first thing trashed to save space in someone's luggage. If people want to see your script, they will normally ask you to send it to their offices.

at the festival

Once you've arrived in Park City, it's a good idea to take some time to familiarise yourself with the locations of key festival venues and, more importantly, how long it takes to get to each one from where you're staying. At certain times of the day, things like traffic and crowds conspire to prevent you from arriving at your destination on time, and the weather can also add insult to injury.

Meetings
Allow plenty of time to get to any meetings you've arranged. It's always better to be early and have time to kill than be late and have to start by apologising. Before you get to your meeting, make sure you've prepared your story so that when you walk through the door, you are calm and confident, and can impress people with your ability to get to the point in an interesting, but speedy, manner. Know what you're going to say, but don't work from a script. You are most effective where you come across naturally, and with a personal touch.

Most formal meetings in Park City will be fairly brief, so it's important to be focused (because it's quite likely the other person won't be). Remember to turn off your mobile phone for the duration of the meeting or, if you're reasonably friendly with the person, decide at the beginning whether it's a "phones on" or "phones off" meeting. If you're meeting someone for the first time, don't be offended if they take calls during the meeting; however, your position in the grand pecking order of the film industry means that you shouldn't take calls yourself.

After the meeting, it's a good idea to take a few minutes and make some notes about what was discussed. Any successful meetings should be followed-up one or two weeks after the festival.

Networking

If you're at Sundance with any type of business agenda, you should be networking as much as you can. This means being forward (but friendly) and striking up a conversation wherever the opportunity presents itself: on the bus, at a party, in one of the official venues, in a line, after a panel event, wherever! It's also important never to be dismissive of someone's ultimate worth. Just because the person is a wannabe now doesn't mean they won't be in a position of power a few years down the road. It's often the people you least expect who end up being the most important for your future.

If you do meet someone interesting, make sure you swap business cards. It's quite common to collect a wad of cards over the course of the festival, so a neat trick is to jot down a note about the person on the back of the card. This is particularly useful for people you meet at parties or other events where alcohol may be flowing freely. That way, the following morning when you're staring at some dude's business card, you won't be scratching your head thinking, "Who the hell was that?"

Sundance Industry Office

For the 2002 festival, Sundance took its first steps toward making the buying and selling experience easier for the growing posse of sales agents and distributors who make the trek to Park City each January. Through the creation of an official festival industry Office, the festival now provides a variety of services for buyers and sellers. These include a service to keep track of film rights and territories which are available for films in the festival program and a centralised meeting place for buyers and sellers to get together. Other services are also provided:

Industry Office Screenings

The Industry Office holds a collection of non-public screenings of films in the festival program. Tickets to Industry Office screenings are available by invitation only.

Video Library

A video library, containing VHS and DVD copies for many of the films in the festival program, is accessible to specially accredited festivalgoers. The library is located at Festival HQ and allows attendees to view festival films on a sign-up basis.

Mailbox Service

A supervised mailbox service for specially accredited festivalgoers is available throughout the event at Festival HQ.

Internet Access

The sales office provides a group of Internet-enabled computers to allow registrants to check email and catch up on the latest Sundance news.

Online Contact Directory

A complete contact directory

is made available to specially accredited festivalgoers to help connect buyers and sellers. Directories are available in early December, shortly after the final film selection is announced.

In addition to these services, the sales office is staffed throughout the festival. It provides information and facilitates networking amongst buyers and sellers to help promote business activity focused on festival films. For more information on the Festival Sales Office and accreditation criteria, contact the Sundance Institute at 801-328-3456 or visit the festival Web site (www.sundance.org).

screening your film

Screening a film in Park City during Sundance has become a dream for many independent filmmakers. Whilst virtually all filmmakers aspire to having their film selected for the Sundance program, many filmmakers over the years have decided to take a DIY approach just to have their film showing in Park City whilst the festival is in town. In the early Sundance days, when the festival was much smaller, the decision to screen in Park City outside the official programs was simpler. However, the reality of Sundance today means that just showing up and projecting a film to a rapturous audience is pretty much a pipe dream.

It's certainly true that Sundance history is peppered with examples of filmmakers who, in the face of rejection, simply jumped on a plane to Utah, created their own *whatever-*

dance, and screened their films in Park City. But this idea has been done to death. Today, there are just too many of these types of pseudo-festivals in Park City, and the sad reality is that, aside from the top one or two, no one cares about them.

Films screening in Park City during the festival tend to fall into a kind of unofficial hierarchy in terms of how much attention they receive from the industry, the press, and festivalgoers themselves. In the top tier, you have the films in the Sundance programs, particularly those in Premieres, competition, and American Spectrum. Films showing in Slamdance sit perhaps one or two tiers down from this, and below these, films screening in Slamdunk and Nodance. As you approach the bottom of the hierarchy, you find films which are screening in other small, unofficial festivals, and finally, at the very bottom, films that are being screened outside any organised event. The reality is that the closer to the bottom of this tier structure your screening is, the harder it will be for you to stand out from the multitude of other films showing in Park City.

This problem of being lost amongst the crowd is compounded by the fact that Sundance is considerably larger than it was in the 1990s, when the whole idea of alternative festivals was really in vogue. For example, in 1993 the festival screened around 140 films in the official program, whereas in 2004, that number was 255. With the size of the Sundance Film Festival today, plus the larger, more-established alternative events, and, of course, all the ambush marketers, resources for screening films of any kind in Park City are stretched to the absolute limit.

Resource issues aside, another key consideration for those thinking of screening a film outside any organised event is whether the film is actually even right for Park City. Before packing your film and buying a flight, you should consider a range of questions: Is the subject matter of the film suited to a Park City audience? Does the film have enough legs to stand above the crowd, or does it run the risk of being lost? Is the film really going to be finished in time, or are you rushing it just to be at Sundance? All these questions are important considerations since going to Sundance just to be in Park City has the potential to harm your film as much as help it. In many cases, screening your film at a smaller festival, where it can make a bigger splash, may foster a better chance of long-term success than having a small screening in Park City, which is missed amongst all of the other hubbub that goes on during Sundance. The bottom line is that it's generally not a good idea to adversely affect a film's chances purely to be in Park City in January.

All of this may sound fairly negative, but the intention is to help you understand the realities of Sundance in the new millennium and draw your attention away from some of the myths that accumulated around the festival during the 1990s. Screening films without representation, outside of any organised event, is a battle that most independent filmmakers will simply struggle to win. It's hard enough for the more marginal films in

the official programs to get exposure, let alone those in the established alternative festivals. If you're not even in any of these events, you really are at the bottom of the "who cares?" pile. And as an independent filmmaker, the last thing you want is a bill for an expensive holiday in a ski resort and nothing to show for it.

Taking all this on board, if you are still hell-bent on screening your film in Park City, but missed out on an official Sundance berth, your best bet is to try and get your film into one of the major alternative festivals. Your chances of collecting any press or acquisitions attention are still very minimal, but at least these events are marketed, focused, and most importantly, they will have nailed down a chunk of Park City's scarcest resource: screening space. Obviously, you still have to be accepted into one of these festivals, but they probably represent your best (and only) chance of getting any benefits from showing your film in Park City during Sundance.

promoting your screening

It doesn't matter whether you are screening in the Sundance program, one of the alternative festivals, or have decided to ignore the perceived wisdom and are planning to show your film in Park City independently: Promoting your screening is absolutely essential if you want any chance of being heard above (or even amongst) the other noise in town during the festival. If you're working with a sales agent and/or publicist, these people are in the best position to advise you on how to develop the most effective campaign for your film.

If you're going it alone, remember that Sundance was the birthplace of independent-film self-promotion, so it's virtually guaranteed that any trick or stunt you can think of has been tried before. So prior to spending a cent on any form of marketing, stop and take a moment to think about exactly who you want to come to your screening. The first rule of marketing is *know your audience*, and if you want to have any success in Park City, you need to know who you're talking to. Assuming you're taking the DIY approach to promotion, your resources are most likely going to be very limited, so it's therefore doubly important that anything you do doesn't miss its target audience.

If your main aim is to try to get your film acquired, then you should be thinking of ways to market to acquisitions executives and the press, not the general public. Marketing to buyers is very different from marketing for a cinema-going audience. If acquisition is the name of the game, spending a huge amount of effort on getting a posse of cinema lovers to show up for your screening is largely a waste of time. Even if the audience likes your film, the chances of such a small number of people creating enough buzz to prick up the ears of buyers is remote, to say the least. On the other hand, if your idea is to hold a screening that will go down in Park City history, you're probably going to need to develop a strong buzz around the screening. You want to focus your energies on building the anticipation amongst your audience and having them spread the word ahead of your premiere.

Strategies for hyping your screening are as limitless as your creativity; however, *unique* and *memorable* should be the two keywords that drive everything that you do. Remember that the second law of marketing applies to hyping films as well: *It's all in the mix*. In other words, there's no one sure-fire thing to do that will result in thousands of people showing up; rather, it's the combination of a bunch of activities that will hopefully achieve the desired results. Here are some suggestions:

Hire Professionals
At a minimum, a sales agent, but ideally a publicist as well. Sales agents take their fees from selling your film, and publicists aren't as expensive as you might think — particularly if they like your film.

Talk to Journalists
Browse the trade magazines, local newspapers, and any other publications that cover the festival. Find the names of journalists who seem to have a style appropriate to your movie and contact them via their magazines to see if they are interested. You will probably be ignored by most of them, but all you need is one or two, and you're in business.

Invite People Personally
Once you have your screenings in place and understand your target audience, do your research and invite the necessary people personally.

The Paper Drop
Each morning, deliver your flyers to any place you see free magazines and other promotional materials (however, please be responsible with your placement). People are suckers for free stuff and will pick up your flyer if it looks interesting enough.

Make it a Premiere
Don't show your film to anyone ahead of the first screening because once you let the cat out the bag, you lose a major advantage.

Postcards
Make sure you always carry a bundle of postcards which have your film's screening time(s) and venue(s) printed on the back. That way, when you meet people in lines, on buses, or around town, and tell them about your film, you have something to give them to help them remember where and when they can see it.

Posters
These are now more difficult than they used to be. Park City officials have understandably become rather sick of filmmaker stunts during Sundance and are now extremely tough on advertising in unapproved places. To help alleviate the problem, the festival itself places free poster boards outside key venues around town for filmmakers to use to promote their films. If you use these boards, you will need to update your posters on a daily basis since other people have no qualms about covering your poster with their own. Besides the poster boards, if you ask nicely

(and patronise their businesses), some shops, bars, or cafés may be happy to display your poster.

These are just a few ideas. The finer points of festival marketing are beyond the scope of this book; there are complete volumes dedicated to the art of getting films noticed at festivals. For more on this subject, check out *Marketing and Selling Your Film Around the World: A Guide for Independent Filmmakers* by John Durie, Annika Pham, and Neil Watson, or *The Ultimate Film Festival Survival Guide* by Chris Gore. Both books are available from the SFVG shop at the official companion Web site for this book (www.sundanceguide.net).

final words of wisdom

Here are a couple of snippets of Sundance advice that will go a long way toward making your Park City experience successful and that much more valuable.

Broaden Your Horizons
With almost 40,000 people in town for the festival, the potential for meeting new and interesting contacts is greater than ever. You should resist the temptation to spend your whole time at Sundance hanging out with your cast and crew, people from your hometown, or even your home country if you're an international visitor. There's no point in making the trek to Park City simply to spend time with people you can see at home. Broaden your horizons and meet people who would otherwise be difficult or impossible to see.

Eyes on the Road
Park City in January is cold, freezing, in fact, and that means any liquid water on the ground quickly turns to ice. Each year, hundreds of festivalgoers receive injuries ranging from bruised egos to broken bones as a result of coming out at the wrong end of an altercation with some pavement ice. Make sure you don't join them by keeping your eyes on the road whenever you're walking around town.

Take Time Out
If you're staying in Park City for the entire festival (or even a good chunk of it), it's important to build some rest time into your schedule. Taking time out clears your head and reinvigorates your love for an industry that can at times feel like it is deliberately out to spite you.

Free Magazines
It's possible to pick up many film magazines for free at various locations around Park City during the festival. These range from industry trades, like *Variety* and *The Hollywood Reporter*, to more fan-orientated publications, like *Entertainment Weekly* or *Premiere*. News and reviews are also available from independent film stalwart *indieWIRE*, which produces a daily print publication in Park City during the festival in addition to its normal online coverage. In 2004, the festival also began publishing the *Sundance Film Festival Daily inSIder*, a free newspaper to help keep you up-to-date with all the important information.

All of these publications can usually be picked up from the theatres and festival venues around town, such as Festival HQ, Sundance House, and the Filmmaker Lodge.

Keep It Real
It's a good idea to make sure you keep your expectations in check if you're trying to sell a film at Sundance. The reality is that only a small number of films get picked up by distributors at the festival each year. These are usually films with recognisable names involved (either in front of or behind the camera) or films which go into Sundance with extremely good buzz. Some films go on to be picked up at other events later in the year, even if deals were talked about in Park City, and sadly, a good many simply fade into the annals of Sundance history, never to be heard of again. All of these scenarios are possibilities you should be prepared to deal with.

Finally...
Tom Clyde at the Park Record suggests the following essential Sundance survival tips:

"1) When in doubt, wear black;

2) No, you can't park there;

3) If the person you are talking to on your cell phone is at the same table, hang up and talk face to face;

4) Yes, the locals think you are from outer space, but it's okay."

Sundance — A Festival Virgin's Guide... out.

the
lowdown

Because Sundance is such an important industry event, a variety of people from across the film world attend it. Although their jobs in Park City can vary dramatically, these people share one thing in common — they were all Sundance virgins at one time, too.

In this section, Sundance veterans from across all walks of the industry share their thoughts and experiences on visiting Park City for the first time and describe how the festival is for them today.

This series of interviews will be expanded at the *Sundance — A Festival Virgin's Guide Web* site as time progresses.

Arianna Bocco

Senior Vice-President of Acquisitions
Miramax Films (New York)

Arianna Bocco joined Miramax Films as Senior Vice-President of Acquisitions in October 2001 and relocated to New York City. For the previous six years, she worked on various acquisitions assignments at New Line Cinema and Fine Line Features, including *The Anniversary Party*, *The Invisible Circus*, and Werner Herzog's *Invincible*. She was also instrumental in acquiring *Trick* and *Saving Grace* for Fine Line. Since joining Miramax, Arianna has been involved in acquiring *Tadpole*, directed by Gary Winick; *DysFunKtional Family*, starring Eddie Griffin; the French romantic comedy *Jet Lag*, directed by Danièlle Thompson; and most recently, the 2003 Sundance Audience Award winner, *The Station Agent*, directed by Tom McCarthy. She also worked on the current release of the Brazilian film *City Of God*.

Previously, Arianna worked at ICM, the Steve Tisch Company, and for writer/director Jeremy Leven on his directorial debut *Don Juan DeMarco*.

BC: When did you lose your "Sundance virginity," and what were your first impressions of the festival?

AB: The first time I went to Sundance, I wasn't actually there for work. In a way, I think that was a good way to lose my "Sundance virginity," so to speak, without the added pressure of having a job to do there as well. I think that year might have been 1996; I had a friend who was a ski instructor, so I went to Park City during the festival and was able to get tickets for some of the screenings. Although I worked for Fine Line Features at the time, I was able to go in a more relaxed environment, which was quite nice because I didn't have to hit the ground in a frenzied state, never having been there before. So when I went the next year for work, it was actually a pleasant experience because I already had a layout of the city; I knew where everything was and how the festival operated.

BC: What were your first impressions of Park City itself? Did you have any preconceptions going in there?

AB: I don't think I really had any preconceptions other than being aware that it was known more for skiing than anything else. I guess I had pictured a kind of ski-lodge-type environment and somewhere that was not quite as busy. Because I'm not from the West — I grew up in New Jersey — I also didn't really know what old mountain mining towns looked like, so I think my first impression was, "It's so quaint and cute." These days, I guess it's still a gorgeous town, but after many trips there, that impression does tend to change. I remember on one of my earlier visits, some of the locals weren't very nice to me. I think there are two types of locals in Park City: the ones who embrace the people that come in, and the ones who can't stand the fact that Hollywood types are there. Unfortunately, I encountered some of the latter one year... people who were simply not happy that I was there in my black jacket, with my cell phone. Somebody actually spat at me, and I was like, "What?!!" I wasn't doing anything — I was just standing on the side of the street. Thankfully it hasn't been repeated since, and despite that experience, I always look forward to going to Park City.

BC: These days, what sort of preparation would you do for Sundance, and how far ahead would you start?

AB: We normally start right after the end of the Toronto Film Festival, which is in the first few weeks of September. When we get back from Toronto, we do a wrap for that festival, part of which includes identifying films we've been tracking which didn't go to Toronto. These get put on a Sundance tracking list. It's also about the same time that you get the registration forms for Sundance, which seems obscenely early, but it also operates as a kind of reminder that Sundance is on the horizon. So pretty much from that point up until they announce the line-up, all of the executives here are calling producers and finding out who's showing what

to Sundance. We look at films all the way up until Christmas — it's really about trying to get a sense of what's on. The tracking process really goes on throughout the entire year, but we focus and try to narrow it down starting after Toronto, more so once they announce the line-up in late November.

We have a database that has thousands of films in it, so once they announce the films, we contact every filmmaker. There are always a few surprises in the selection, films that we've never heard of before or very low-budget films that were made under the radar, but we basically try and contact each filmmaker directly. Because filmmakers are more savvy these days and know they need representation, a lot of them are trying to get reps to help sell their films at the same time. It can be a very busy period. Sometimes filmmakers are really surprised to hear from us, but it's our job to know everything about the film before going in: things like who produced it, who directed it, who's in it, what it's about, and how it might fit into our slate. It's important for us to be able to walk in, even though we haven't actually seen the movie, knowing what every aspect of the film is about.

BC: These films that you are tracking, do they tend to fall into one type or another — for example, things that are more name driven (either in front of or behind the camera) — or is it really just across the board?

AB: It's pretty much across the board; however, films that go to Sundance tend to be more on the American independent level. The festival generally gets a good cross section of documentaries and a good selection of world cinema, but in the two years I've been at Miramax, the three films we've bought out of Sundance were very-American independent films. And that's not a bad thing — Sundance is really the one festival for the showcase of independent American cinema — but of course some years are better than others. I think one of the criticisms many people have had about Sundance in recent years is that it now caters to movie stars, but my feeling is that it's an amazing opportunity for some of these actors to do films they normally wouldn't get a chance to do.

BC: Once you arrive in Park City, how does a typical day tend to pan out for you during the festival?

AB: Sundance is 10 days, and they break it up into two parts in terms of the film schedules and the ticket situation. For us, the first week is generally the busiest because they show the most films during those first five days. And the majority of the day is really spent seeing movies. I normally get an Express Pass, which is really lucky because they're very expensive, so I can go to pretty much any movie I want to see.

We have quite a few executives at the festival, so at the beginning of the day, we'll all sit down and do a schedule of who's going to see which films. Depending on what people think of those films, this can also involve scheduling second screenings. So really my day is all about seeing movies — as many movies as I can. That can also mean that there are often times when you

don't eat or you're eating on the fly in order to leave as much time as possible for the films. Even if you don't end up buying them, you really want to spend some time meeting the filmmakers because they're all there, and it's such a great meeting place.

In the second week, you usually have a little more downtime because the festival schedule starts to repeat the films, and you will have seen a lot of them by that point. So you try and arrange more meetings with people during this time and go to less screenings.

BC: So how many films do you think you'd see in an average festival?

AB: You know, I stopped counting. When I first started, it was cool to count how many films, but now I've really stopped. I think the most intense festival is actually Cannes because it's a market and a festival in one, whereas at Sundance, you can be a little bit more selective. I guess I just try to see as many films as one can fit into a day, depending on the schedule. You're often in a midnight screening at Sundance, and you can hear the party raging next door. Fortunately, I'm kind of over the whole Sundance party thing.

BC: Is it common for acquisitions people to meet with producers at Sundance, or do you deal mainly with sales agents?

AB: Both. We deal a lot with producers, but it ultimately depends on the project. Sometimes, if you don't have a relationship with a certain filmmaker, it's nice to have that introduction through a sales agent.

BC: Acquisitions deals at Sundance tend to get a lot of press. Is it common for these to be finalised at Sundance, or are the deals completed later down the track?

AB: If you're interested in a film and you want to buy it, then you need to do it right then and there. Those stories about sitting in a room all night negotiating are true. You really have to close the deal at that moment because the level of competition is so extreme. Sometimes sales agents have different plans for the deal and will try to drag it out in order to get a better price, but from our point of view, once you've agreed you want it, you have to sit down and hash it out right then and there.

BC: What's the craziest thing you've had a filmmaker do to try and attract your attention as an acquisitions person?

AB: Well, this one guy kind of stalked me a little bit. I would be sitting in a restaurant, and I'd hear my name behind me. I would turn around, and he would be there waving at me. Somehow he also managed to get my cell-phone number and would call me quite frequently, too. We'd already seen his movie and decided that it wasn't something for us, and I'd told him that, but he didn't seem to get it. It was bordering on that level of, "Do I do something about this?" Fortunately, I think he ultimately got the message. Other than that, I can't really think of anything completely crazy. Plenty of filmmakers do pull stunts to try and promote their films to the acquisitions people in town, but I can't think of anything really crazy.

BC: Historically, Sundance has been known as a very American festival. How important is it for international films these days?

AB: It seems to be becoming more important for international distributors. A lot more have been attending the festival in recent years and buying up the popular films for their territories. I think that's a good thing for the festival, but it's really the filmmakers who benefit because their films are getting more international attention. I think independent films on the whole are doing a lot better all over the world these days — there are more distributors who are willing to handle them, and there's more variety out there. We bought *The Station Agent* last year [2003], and Alliance Atlantis [from Canada] came in right after and picked up international on it, which was great for that movie.

BC: Is it common for a company like Miramax to go after worldwide rights, or is it more likely that you would do deals like you did with Alliance on *The Station Agent*, where Miramax takes the U.S. rights, and you then work with a foreign distributor for the other rights?

AB: We do all sorts of deals — there's no one formula. We picked up other territories for *The Station Agent*, and we handled the international distribution in some territories ourselves. Every film is different, and the type of deal really depends on the film.

BC: How much attention do you think that the industry pays to these alternative festivals that take place at the same time as Sundance?

AB: Unfortunately, not a lot. It's mainly a time issue, but it can also be a "quality of the films" issue. The one festival we do pay attention to and we do attend is Slamdance because there have been films which have sold at that festival. Slamdance has been around longer, and because they're filmmakers themselves, they know and understand how it all works. Days go by very quickly during the festival so you have to prioritise your time, and there's just not enough of it for the other fringe festivals. In some ways, I think it's a mistake for filmmakers to think that they can go to Park City in one of these events, show their film, and get people's attention. It's just not a reality in my opinion.

BC: Do you have any memorable Sundance anecdotes?

AB: [laughs] Unfortunately, some of the really memorable ones, I can't put into print for fear of damaging my reputation. But in all the films I've been involved with buying at Sundance, I've definitely had some good times. It can be pretty heady in the sense of there being a real adrenaline rush when you get into a room and you want to buy a film. I think all of the negotiations for the films I've been involved with were not only intense but you formed certain bonds with people. We'd call it "being in the trenches" because it can be really intense, kind of fun and exhilarating, stressful, and sometimes even disastrous, all at the same time.

One particular example was the first year I went to Sundance with Miramax. We bought *Tadpole*, and that was a huge bidding war. I had previously worked at Fine Line Features in L.A. and had just moved to Miramax in New York. We were bidding in the sales agent's condo which was massive and had three floors. We were in the basement, and Fine Line was on the top floor. It was a little bit nerve racking during the negotiation knowing that my compadres were also in the building — I almost felt like a traitor. On one hand, it was kind of fun bidding against each other, but on the other, a bit nerve racking.

How we got to that point is an interesting story too... Basically, after the screening of *Tadpole*, Mark Gill and I decided that we really, really liked the movie, and we wanted to find the director right then and there and talk to him. But he had already left for dinner, and no one knew which restaurant he had gone to. So we literally walked from the Library all the way to the top of Main Street, going into every single restaurant looking for him. We eventually found him on the way back down, kind of crashed his dinner, and talked with him for a bit. I think he was a bit surprised at first, but then he welcomed it. Sometimes you really have to do things to show people that you really loved the movie, and often that's what filmmakers respond to.

BC: When you're not crashing filmmakers' dinners, do you have any favourite places to eat in Park City?

AB: There are those two breakfast places on Main Street — the Morning

Ray Café and Bakery and The Eating Establishment. Those are the best breakfast places. I also love the Thai restaurant on Main Street — Bangkok Thai, I think it's called. Grappa is always great, but most of the time, I find myself eating really disgusting muffins from Albertsons. You know the funny thing is, Albertsons is really the meeting place for everyone on the first day of the festival — that's a secret not many people know. If you want to meet a lot of Hollywood production people or distributors, go to Albertsons and cruise the aisles. On the first day, everybody is there getting food for their condos.

BC: From what you said previously about your hectic screening schedule, I guess you don't have that much time for networking and socialising. When you do get a spare moment, are there any particular places you prefer to go?

AB: Usually if I have some spare time, I've got to catch up on work or office stuff, so the places I tend to end up socialising in are either restaurants, when I bump into people, or at industry-sponsored parties.

BC: Do you have any general advice for future Sundance virgins?

AB: I would say the best advice, especially for filmmakers, is to keep your head about you because it can be a very exhilarating place where there's not much reality happening. Films always screen better at Sundance than they will in a movie theatre. You're going to get attention from everyone, from agents to producers to distributors, but sometimes that attention can be incredibly fleeting. I think people can get on a real high when they're there, and it's not just the lack of oxygen. It's incredible to be in a place where there's a lot of great talent — people you've always wanted to meet — but you have to keep things in perspective.

Prioritisation is also important. If there are three producers you want to meet, then don't worry yourself with the rest of what's going on until you have that sorted. Try to focus on meeting those three producers. And have something to talk about. A lot of people just want to meet you, but they don't really have anything to say. Go there with a plan. I think the worst thing to do, unless you just want to go skiing and have fun, is show up in Park City without a plan.

Linda Brown-Salomone
Publicist
Indie PR (Los Angeles)

Linda Brown is a veteran film and television publicist who has successfully represented hundreds of films and television programs and organized countless industry parties at Sundance and other key events. Linda's career began at the famed PMK Public Relations in Los Angeles, where she handled celebrities, films, production companies, and television shows. She launched the internationally acclaimed animated TV series, The Simpsons, and remained with it for the show's first four years. Her celebrity clients have included Winona Ryder, Andie MacDowell, Nicolas Cage, Christian Slater, Rosanne Barr, and Richard Pryor. While at PMK, she worked on such critically acclaimed films as My Left Foot and La Femme Nikita. Later, Linda became Vice-President for Motion Pictures for the West Coast office of Rogers & Cowan, where she worked on campaigns for a range of Hollywood studio movies, including The Mask, Young Guns II, Double Dragon, and National Lampoon's Loaded Weapon.

Linda is now a founding partner of Indie PR. Creating the firm gave Linda a chance to combine her love for independent film with her talent and know-how and help "the underdog" along the way. Presently, she works with a number of studios, including Paramount, Paramount Classics, Artisan, Sony Pictures Entertainment, and Screen Gems, and also continues to fulfil her mission in the independent world. Indie PR is one of the most sought-after firms to represent both art and independent films on the festival circuit.

BC: When did you lose your Sundance virginity, and what were your first impressions of the festival?

LBS: I've been doing the festival for about nine years now... To tell you the truth, I don't remember my very first experience at Sundance; I think I went up with a client — it may have been Andie MacDowell for a movie; I'm not quite sure. But I went up as a talent representative, which is a very different experience to going up and representing films as a publicist. I remember my first experience as a talent rep being quite pleasant, but as a publicist, it was a little bit more insane. You don't tend to remember any of it when you get home — all you know is that one of your movies won an award, or one of your movies was more successful to a degree than another... you just kind of forget the process and remember the rewards.

BC: And what about Park City itself?

LBS: The first time I went there was quite a long time ago, and it was a completely different experience to how it is today. The festival was not as crazy as it is now; it was easy to get a reservation for a restaurant, easy to get a hotel, and all that stuff. I think it's become a bit of a "dog and pony" show these days with all this corporate sponsorship and these people running around who have no rhyme or reason for being there filmwise. On my first visit, it was more about the independent filmmaker, but it was shortly thereafter that it started to get a little bit more studio and corporate driven. My first experience was a very indie experience because all of the films there were independent... actually, I think it was the year that *sex, lies and videotape* broke... that was more than nine years ago, wasn't it?

BC: Yeah, it was 1989.

LBS: [laughs] Well, I'd like to lie about my age and say I was still in grammar school in 1989, but I think that was actually my first festival experience. *Sex, lies and videotape* kind of made Soderbergh a star, and it was exciting to see all of that stuff going on around me, but it was very much an indie experience.   Everybody wanted to know all about independent filmmaking, and the sorts of questions that were fired at people were along the lines of, "What's it like working on an indie film versus a studio film? How much more rewarding is it?" and so on. Whereas now when you go the festival with a star of some notoriety who's done studio films, it just tends to turn into a junket. The questions aren't as interesting, the interviews are all held for the film's release, and you kind of wonder why they're even happening.

BC: What sort of preparation do you do these days before you arrive in Park City?

LBS: Well, it really depends on the type of project you are taking to the festival. For example, yesterday I had a screening for the shorts programmers of this film I'm hoping to get into the festival — this short that's been made with the help of a new technology Kodak has developed. On one side, I guess I kind of feel like I'm betraying the indie spirit because the project is Kodak driven, but on the other side, the director is a first-timer to the film arena (he's done some TV projects before), so this film is really his baby.

In terms of what I did for this short, at this point, we're very much in the beginning stages of the programmers' look at the movie. I try to get to the programmers sooner, rather than later, to set up a very formal screening where they can come along and be educated about what's going on with the film and the technology. In this case, I've been telling them about how Kodak is looking to use Sundance as a platform to launch the new technology, and this may or may not entice them to include it. If the programmers are on the fence about it, maybe this will help push them over the edge, but then maybe it won't. I guess the most important thing is to get to them early, before all the craziness starts, because as the deadlines get closer, they don't have time to get out to a screening.

BC: Is it common for publicists to arrange screenings for the programmers ahead of the festival?

LBS: Is it common? If you get to them early enough, I think it's done, but I don't know if it's so common. I do think it is refreshing for the programmers to hear from a publicist rather than a producer's rep who's trying to sell the movie and therefore has a monetary interest in getting it into the festival; or from a studio, who is simply calling because they want to world-premiere a film that's being released three weeks later, saying, "We'll throw a big junket," etc. I think to get a call from someone like me who's an independent publicist, whose interests are mainly about trying to make a difference for a movie, is more refreshing than someone who is simply interested in selling something.

I get such satisfaction up at the festival when it all works out. Last year, we had a movie called *Soldier's Girl* — a true story based on this guy who was in the military who fell in love with a transgendered performer. I knew about the story and fell in love with the movie, so I got in touch with Kenny Turan (of the *Los Angeles Times*) early — again, early, that's the key word here — I got to him early and said, "Look, Kenny, if you respond to this movie, I'd love for you to include something about it in your opening day's story at Sundance," because that really gets the ball rolling with a campaign. Having a movie highlighted in a *Los Angeles Times* opening-day story means so much: it perks up the ears of the distributors, it perks up the ears of the critics, and it fills the first screening with everybody.

So I try to get to key opinion makers like Kenny Turan early, and in this case, not only did Kenny include it in his opening-day story, it ended up getting a feature in the paper on day four of the festival with loads of pictures and interviews. The movie did so well as a result of that.

BC: How does a typical day in Park City tend to pan out for you during the festival?

LBS: We normally get there the day before the festival to set up our office... and we really do move almost our entire office up to Sundance for the 10 days of the festival. Once we're there, things are pretty much going on non-stop for the entire time. On a typical day, we would wake up, look at the columns and the papers, and also the clipping service, to find out what ran, if anything of ours ran. Then we finalise our schedules for the day, and the schedules of the directors and actors we are working with. We try to fill their day with interviews to try and help sell a movie. There's so much press in Park City during the festival, and our job is to use them to help get distributors interested in the movie.

BC: So the publicity is really targeted at the acquisitions people — the buyers — rather than the general public?

LBS: Yes. The general public will get the publicity at the time of release, so you're really targeting the buyers at this point. At the festival, there's a huge amount of noise, so it's important to scream louder than anyone else, and the more you get into these stories every day, the more loudly you are screaming. It's really important for the distributors to be aware of your movie so that once they arrive in Park City, they instantly recognise the title.

My job really starts early on with those opening-day stories because people are reading the *Los Angeles Times* on the plane to Park City. The local papers are equally important because they're in the front of your hotel when you check in. People somehow think that if it's on the front page of the *Park Record* and it's mentioned in Kenny Turan's opening-day story, if they don't see the film, then they're going to miss out on something. So they make sure it's on their schedule of films to see at the festival, and that's most of my job done.

At that point, I hand over to the rep and the producer — it's their job to sell the movie. My job is to get the buyers in there, get the press to do good reviews...not that I can actually force the press to do good reviews, but I can concentrate on getting the right critic to the right film so hopefully they can review the film positively. It's then that the acquisition people come out of the woodwork. So that's really my job, the first stage of sales.

BC: If you were going to represent a film at Sundance, what sort of materials would you expect the filmmakers to have produced for you?

LBS: It's especially important to have a strong photo, one that really represents what the movie is about. So many times I see, in the festival programs and things like that, some

kind of talking-head picture, and then occasionally something will catch my eye because the photo is different. Like everyone says, it's worth a thousand words, and if you've got a great photo that catches the eye, then people will notice your movie. When someone is putting together their schedule of movies to see, and your photo catches their eye, they're like, "Oh, that looks kind of interesting." So if you have a celebrity in your movie, throw the celebrity's picture in there, but an interesting picture. Even if you don't have a celebrity, just throw in some kind of interesting picture. Ideally you want to have a still photographer on set taking these photos for you, but if you can't afford a photographer (which is usually the first thing to go along with publicity when you're cutting the budget), it is possible to pull a frame off the film. In the world of digital today, you can probably pull something off the Avid and turn it into a photo, but the results are never as good as having a decent photographer take the shot on set.

As far as a press kit goes, you want to have a couple of stills, at least one image that people instantly recognise that you can make into a poster or postcards. Postcards are very important at a festival, postcards which have the time, date, and location of your screening printed on the back. If you run into Roger Ebert at Starbucks on Main Street, get into a really interesting conversation with him about your movie, he's genuinely interested, and then you go, "Oh, my screening's at blah blah blah at three o'clock....," he's not going to remember that. You need something to hand him, an interesting image; flip it over, and there is the information on how to contact you and when and where your screenings are. At the end of the night, everybody empties their pockets onto their dresser, and the next morning, they pick up your postcard, and it says to them, "I met this interesting person last night, and I really want to go to this movie."

In terms of the rest of the press kit, I usually write the press kit for a lot of independent filmmakers because they just don't know how to do it. A press kit at a festival is very different to one you give out to the media during a film's release. The release kits are very intense, with full credits and all that stuff. At Sundance, all they want to know is who directed it and who stars in it because the chances of getting a feature article about your movie are so minimal unless there's some kind of unique story behind it. You tend to get included in these roundup stories, which are extremely important, but it's always just snippets of information. If the journalist writing these stories has to sift through 25 pages of, "My grandmother lent me the money," "I cashed in my savings bonds," they just don't care. Everybody cashes in their bonds; everybody's grandmother invests in the movie...it's an old story; nobody cares. So I usually interview the filmmaker and try to find an angle that's different, and then I write the press kit based around that.

BC: You touched on strategies for raising awareness of a film in Park City a little earlier... are there any that tend to work better than others?

LBS: Again, I just think the key is getting to a publicist early — even before you're accepted into a festival. If you wait until after you're accepted, it's not too late, but it's always a good idea to give the publicist a heads-up that you're submitting to Sundance and have them look at it so that they can hit the ground running, so to speak. For example, with this short I'm doing, regardless of whether the movie gets into Sundance or not, this technology is new, and Kodak will be announcing it at the festival, so it's not a bad idea for me to start with magazines like *Premiere*, *RES*, and *FILMMAKER* to try and get some features on this movie which will break during Sundance. These magazines have a very high profile at the festival, but there is a three-month lead time for getting into them. So if the movie ends up getting in, it's icing on the cake because these magazines will be read by people in Park City, and that's three more shouts if it's in the festival.

BC: How much attention does the industry pay to films that are playing in the alternative festivals such as Slamdance?

LBS: I think that Slamdance has really grown and come into its own to a certain degree. I had a movie called *Man of the Century* that played in Slamdance a few years ago which won the Audience Award. I think if you go after an award, and you actually receive an award at one of these festivals, ears tend to prick up and people are like, "Oh, this movie performed at Slamdance; it's probably worth taking a look." In the case of *Man of the Century*, Fine Line ended up acquiring the movie. The film had been turned down by Sundance, and we only came on board three days before the festival. We had to scramble to write a press kit, get the filmmakers together, and put together a campaign to target the Audience Award in the event.

Even so, nobody [of any industry importance] came to the screenings in Park City. One of the downsides of Slamdance is that it's a little hard to watch a movie there because of the conditions of the screening rooms. There are folding chairs, you're often sandwiched in a hot room, and people are making lots of noise. I think the studios know that they don't need to go to events like Slamdance; they maybe send a third- or fourth-tier person to check out a movie they might be interested in because they know for the most part, nobody's going to be acquired at those festivals. And if something does end up performing, or if they read a really good review or hear buzz about a film, they'll simply send for it when they get back to L.A. The people who actually write the cheques are way too busy at Sundance to worry about any of the ancillary festivals.

BC: Yeah. There are so many films in the official programs it's not really surprising that the studios don't have a lot of time for other films showing in Park City.

LBS: Absolutely. And sometimes even screening at Sundance itself perhaps isn't the best idea. I saw a movie a couple of nights ago and said to the filmmaker, "You know what? I'd question whether Sundance is the best festival for this movie. I think it would possibly do better in a smaller festival where it can be heard a little louder, like SXSW, LAFF, or the

Hollywood Film Festival." Of course, the filmmaker was, "But I want to go to Sundance!"

I do wonder sometimes whether it's a mistake for a film to be in Sundance just because it's Sundance — it's so hard to get people's attention. I knew a journalist who was a well-known film writer for a major national newspaper who said to me last year, "I'm just going to Park City to ski." And I said, "Well, how do I get anything into your paper?" And they were like, "I'm just going up and skiing. I might see a couple of movies, but I'm just coming to ski." That can be very frustrating because we're sitting there trying to get some play, and this person is worrying about which days they're going to ski and which parties they're going to. They're more interested in my party list than my films!

I also find it frustrating that, compared to years gone by, there seems to have been a cut in magazine space across the board. When I handled *Bloody Sunday* in 2002, we did so much press, but two months later, when the magazines came out with their festival coverage, there was almost nothing on the film. *Bloody Sunday* won the World Cinema Audience Award that year, and *Premiere* magazine did two back-to-back Sundance issues where they highlighted the festival for six pages in each, and *Bloody Sunday* wasn't even mentioned. And when I tell you we did loads of publicity, we did! I had everyone from the magazine see the movie, and they loved it. They photographed the film's star James Nesbitt, they photographed the director Paul Greengrass...yet nothing got in.

Do you know what *did* get in? Anything gay, anything gritty and weird (and quite frankly, unwatchable), and big stars. It's like, "Okay. You're *Premiere* magazine — you're a film magazine. I don't understand why I'm not getting anything into your magazine about an Audience Award winner." Then, of course, you open the magazine, and Britney Spears' appearance on Main Street gets a photo. That's really how the festival has changed: You get people up there who have no reason being there, like J.Lo and Ben Affleck. Okay, Ben has Project Greenlight, but suddenly it's all about J.Lo, and there's a three-page spread in every magazine, and you're just sitting there wondering, "What about the winner of the festival?"

BC: Yeah. I know that this "ambush marketing" has started to become a real problem.

LBS: It just makes my job impossible. In the beginning of my career at Sundance, I was doing a lot of indie movies; I took them on; I was passionate. We killed ourselves trying to get press for the movies and filmmakers we loved. And now nothing runs because Britney Spears is in town. It can be really frustrating. And you know what the sad result of this is? People like myself watch a movie, and we find ourselves thinking, "Well there's no stars, so what can we really do at Sundance?" I try not to think like that, and I usually don't, but sometimes you can't help but have it in the back of your mind when you're watching a movie. It shouldn't be that way.

BC: Do you have an anecdote that you're fond of recounting over the dinner table when the topic of Sundance comes up?

LBS: I remember kidnapping Roger Ebert — literally kidnapping him and dragging him to a screening one time. He was going, "I don't have time... I've got to go... I've got to file..." and I was like, "No, you have to come." That was actually for *Man of the Century*, and he ended up really getting behind the film, so much so that he mentioned it in his column, and that's how Fine Line heard about it.

I have another story...it was a short called *Angry Men*, which was also in Slamdance. The producer had created a whole bunch of fake parking tickets with an invite and the film's screening times printed on the back. He stuck them on cars along Main Street and around town, and the Park City officials went crazy. This was the first year they started seriously cracking down on the noise on Main Street. They got hold of one of his tickets, hunted him down, and threatened to arrest him for impersonating an officer. He called me and asked, "What do I do?" I said, "Let them arrest you. I'm going to have "Page Six" [of the *New York Post*] down there, and we're going to get coverage on this." So he let them arrest him, and "Page Six" was there to cover it, and they ran an item. Off the back of the "Page Six" article, he got a call from MTV, who wanted to have a meeting to discuss making *Angry Men* into a series. It never did quite come to fruition, but it's that sort of experience that makes my job fun.

I want to tell you one more... I was there in 1998 with *20 Dates*; again, this is a Slamdance story because with those you need to be so much more creative. Myles Berkowitz was the director, and Tia Carrere had maybe a minute of screen time in the film. I said to Myles, "I need Tia to come up and do some publicity," and he was like, "There's other things that we could probably do." I insisted that "I just need Tia up there to do the big stuff, and we can figure out the rest." So Myles came up with this idea to bribe every single cabdriver in Park City to put up postcards of the movie all over the cabs and to talk about it as if they'd seen it and loved it. He was like, "Here's a hundred bucks; talk about my movie." And they did. We would hear back from press people who would say, "I heard about this great movie from this cabdriver..." We also sprinkled people on the shuttle busses to talk about the movie and just say, "I saw that movie *20 Dates* at Slamdance, man... it's so much fun." And you know, there's Roger Ebert or the *Premiere* magazine writer, or there's the critic from the *Los Angeles Times*, and they're like, "Which movie did you love?" Because they like to hear from people what they liked.

BC: Do you have any favourite places you like to eat when you're in Park City?

LBS: My condo. When I tell you that I simply go from the office to my room at the end of the day — that's exactly it. It's almost like downloading onto a diskette — I just need to download my brain during that dinner hour, unless I'm working something.

There's also a Chinese restaurant downstairs on Main Street that I like, but I don't want to tell people about it because then all of a sudden, it will be crowded, and I won't be able to get a reservation. That's already a problem: One year, we went down there, and we wanted to eat, we were starving and didn't have a lot of time, but the restaurant was fully booked. There were six of us, so one of us went down and managed to glance at the reservation list, and there was a reservation for six at eight o'clock. It was about 7:45 at this time, so we called the restaurant and said, "We have a reservation in the name of..." — you know, the name that was on the list — "and we're not going to be able to make it." And then the restaurant gave our group the table. That's what you have to do sometimes to get a reservation in Park City!

BC: What about networking and socialising? Are there any places that are better for that sort of thing than others?

LBS: I just think you need to go to the parties. Not so much the Sundance-sponsored parties, but the hot parties like the *Daily Variety* "10 Directors to Watch" party, which is always filled with the people that you should be talking to. The Showtime party is always a staple; the Miramax party is also always hard to get into, but if you can, everyone's there. The magazine parties, like *Entertainment Weekly* and *Premiere*, are always really fun, although you'll probably see more celebrities there than anything. The real networking parties are the ones that are held every year, like *Daily Variety*, Showtime, Miramax — those kinds of parties.

BC: Do you have any general advice for future Sundance virgins, particularly filmmakers?

LBS: Come prepared. You have one shot, so you better be prepared. It's like a big audition — you've got one shot — because if your movie falls on deaf ears at Sundance for whatever reason, six months down the line, when you're in the Hollywood Film Festival, the studios are going to hear about your movie and go, "Hasn't that been around for a while?" The movie starts to feel old in the eyes of the buyers. So go out big, go out with somebody who knows how to make noise about your movie — a really creative producer's rep if you can't afford a publicist, or a publicist that knows what the hell they're doing. It will probably be the best money you'll spend at the festival. I'm sure anybody who gets hired for whatever reason will say that, but I really believe it because I've seen how I've made a difference in a sale by what I've done.

Tina Gharavi
Producer/Director (U.K.)

Tina Gharavi is an award-winning writer/director educated in the United States and France and currently based in the north of England. Since 1996, she has worked as a screenwriter, with several short scripts commissioned and produced. In 2002, she was awarded a U.S. National Endowment for the Arts (NEA) residency. Her recent projects have dynamically blended documentary and fiction-film techniques focused on social issues. These projects have broadcast on TV and screened at many international festivals, including Sundance and International Documentary Festival Amsterdam (IDFA). She has recently been commissioned by U.K. broadcaster Channel 4 to produce *Mother/Country*, a docudrama about returning to Iran 20 years after the Islamic Revolution.

In Newcastle her production company, Bridge + Tunnel Productions, has established KOOCH, a Persian cinema group which will be trained in aspects of media production while collaborating through workshops with Gharavi on a feature script about the experiences of Iranians living in Tyneside (a classic Geordie/Persian romantic comedy staring Omid Djalili).

BC: Your documentary *Closer* was at the 2001 Sundance Film Festival. Was that your first trip to Sundance?

TG: It was, yes.

BC: What were your first impressions of Park City?

TG: It had an amazingly "small-town America" atmosphere to it. It felt very authentic in terms of not being a place where you would instantly assume media moguls would congregate. It really did have the feel of a small community, and for me that was evident from the very beginning because I stayed with a local family while I was at the festival, rather than in a hotel or condo full of 20 people. The family was actually one of the doctors who practice in the town, and so I was able to get a feel for the real lives of people in Park City.

BC: And how did you find the festival itself?

TG: Well, to start with, I have a mortal fear of festivals — I really hate them. I'd already done quite a number of major festivals with *Closer*, and although I realise it's important to get out there and promote your film, make contacts, etc., it's just not something I enjoy at all. But I have to say that Sundance was the only festival I would really like to go back to, mainly because it was one of the rare festivals that really cared about the filmmakers. At most of the other large festivals I'd been to — like IDFA, London, Edinburgh — the filmmaker was paid very little attention to. It wasn't about us giving these festivals something; rather, the festivals were somehow taking something from the films. When I went to Sundance, it was very much about the filmmaker being at the centre of the festival. Filmmakers were given access to different networks that could help them or support them on their trip there, and even for short filmmakers, that idea was carried through. They did a fantastic job of not making shorts feel like just a tag-on. I think that's incredibly important because when you go to big festivals as a shorts director, you often feel like you're just a hanger-on. Everyone at Sundance did an excellent job of making us feel really welcome.

BC: Knowing that you had a film showing in the official program, what sort of preparation did you do ahead of the festival?

TG: The major thing is of course accommodation because you find out that you've been selected quite late. I think I found out that my film had been accepted in December, and by that time, all of the cheap accommodation was already gone. That left me in a very difficult situation because obviously I couldn't afford $150 a night to be out there. I actually ended up writing

a charming email explaining that I'd saved up all my milk money to make a film, that somehow it had gotten into Sundance, but I couldn't afford to go, and did anyone know of some cheap accommodation. I sent this to a lot of the property owners who were on the list suggested to us by Sundance. Virtually none of them wrote back, but one family said, "Our apartment is already rented out, but would you like to come and stay in our house...for free?" So I ended up staying with an amazing family just outside of Park City, in the most amazing house, in the most amazing landscape. I had a hire car, so I could drive into Park City in about 20 minutes along these windy mountain roads, and that was great.

BC: Once you arrived in Park City, how did a typical day tend to pan out for you?

TG: It's a couple of years ago now, so I don't remember everything, but I did spend a bit of time at the House of Docs [now Filmmaker Lodge], where there was a fantastic program of discussions and screenings and a lot of great documentary people. I saw Errol Morris speak there, which was really great because *Closer* was part documentary and part fiction. There were literally loads of things to do, and I didn't have much spare time — you have to manage your time pretty well there because there's a lot going on. I was also quite fortunate because I knew a couple of people who were working at the festival, so I was able to get a lot of invitations to things. It's definitely good to know somebody who works there because that helps with hearing about things that are happening and what parties to go to, but I guess you can also find a lot of that sort of thing out by asking around.

BC: How was it that *Closer* actually came to be selected for the festival?

TG: The film had won an award from Planet Out/iFilm on the Internet. Shari Frilot, who is one of the Sundance programmers, was a judge for the Planet Out competition, and in fact it was she who recommended that I submit it to Sundance. I would never have done that myself because *Closer* is quite experimental, and I'd never imagined that it would have been accepted. I wouldn't have thought of Sundance as a festival that takes experimental stuff... sure, independent stuff, but I thought it would be a lot more traditional or narrative based. So I sent the film in, and it was accepted.

BC: What was involved in preparing to screen the film at the festival?

TG: Well, I did the thing that I guess most filmmakers do, which is putting together some posters. I think our posters really stood out because we got some really good comments back. I'd worked with a Japanese photographer in Paris, who had taken some photos of the subject of my documentary, a girl named Annelise Roger. The photographer had used medium-format stock and then blown the photos up to glossy poster-size prints, and onto these I put a clear sticky label with the name of the film. So these posters really jumped out. I think that's what you've got to do — come up with something that really stands out — because you're competing against so much. I

mean, there are posters everywhere, postcards on the walls; it's just an information overload. So you need to find something which is almost "quieter," if that makes any sense. I think that's what was successful about our posters, this larger image of our girl sitting in quite an amazing pose, looking at the audience.

Other than that, you just have to basically talk to people about your film and get them to come to your screenings. I usually just talked to anyone who I was sitting next to, and that was one of the great things about Sundance. You don't know who you're going to be sitting next to, and you can strike up conversations with people really easily and start talking about your film. I think that worked to bring in some people who otherwise may not have come.

BC: Did you do a post-screening Q&A for your film, and were there any interesting questions?

TG: I did do the Q&A, and it was a great discussion actually. I do remember that after the second screening, the Q&A was really, really animated. Because my director of photography, who's reasonably well known in the industry — he shot parts of *Buffalo 66* and *I Shot Andy Warhol* — just happened to drop in that day. So I got the audience to ask us both questions, and we got into a really good discussion about the film.

BC: Did *Closer* get shown amongst a bunch of other shorts, or did it get stuck on the front of a feature?

TG: It was shown in a program called Frontier Shorts, which is a series of "experimental" films. Ours was the most narrative based out of all of them — there were a lot of very experimental works, such as films that used no images at all, sometimes just texture or colours. Ours was also quite long in comparison — it's 24 and a half minutes — so it was always the last or second-last in the series. Actually, by that time people were probably looking for some narrative, and I think that made ours perhaps seem more narrative based than it actually is.

BC: How did the audience actually receive it? Did it go down well at that point?

TG: It went down really well. It was an amazing reception, and I had loads of people come up to me and say very kind things about it afterward. And also travelling around Park City, I would sometimes have people come up and say, "I saw your film and really liked it a lot." That kind of stuff was also really nice.

BC: You've touched on a couple of anecdotes already...are there any others which stick in your mind?

TG: It mainly has to do with the landscape, to be honest. I lived in America for a long time, most of my life actually, but I've been living in England for the last seven years. I grew up outside of New York, so it's nothing like Utah, but I found that the landscape around Park City just made a huge impact on the experience. I didn't anticipate really how blown away I would be by seeing the flat horizon and these massive mountains. That was so breathtaking. You never see the horizon in England — everything's

so tiny and condensed, so just going to Utah and having that sense of monumental landscape and real open space just put the experience in a different context. And then to have this incredibly nurturing festival where I had the least amount of sense that people were being arrogant or elitist was just amazing.

BC: Did you find any favourite places to eat in Park City?

TG: Yeah, there was this really charming diner on the edge of town, but I can't remember what the name of it was. Perhaps people can ask around. You probably need a car to get there, and it's a kind of very traditional 1900s silver-carriage diner. They have American pancake-style breakfasts and traditional diner food, which is great. There are also some good sushi places on Main Street, and Robert Redford's restaurant [Zoom] is nice as well.

BC: What about places to hang out and/or socialise? Did you find yourself gravitating toward one more than another?

TG: It was mainly the House of Docs that I spent a lot of time in. I also think the Digital Center was nice because it was quite low key and had computers where you could check your email.

BC: After having your film in the official program and being a first-timer yourself, would you have any general advice for future Sundance virgins?

TG: I'd say that probably the key things are 1) go with some well-thought-through publicity. Try to think of a campaign that's different — everyone else is going to have postcards, everyone else is going to have posters, so you have to be really different to get any attention. 2) Try to meet some key people who work at the festival, or certainly meet other people who are in the know about where to be.   3) Stay with locals if you can and try to avoid sleeping 20 people in a hotel room because that's just going to cause unnecessary stress. Finally, enjoy the landscape and try to think of the trip as a retreat... a filmmaker's retreat.

Gary Hamilton
Managing Director
Arclight Films (Australia)

Gary Hamilton is a veteran of more than 20 years in international film sales. His achievements include founding Beyond Films in 1990, which he helmed for 12 years. During this time, he amassed for the Beyond library more than 150 titles, including early starring roles for Russell Crowe, Heath Ledger, and Cate Blanchett. Prior to that, Gary was well known in the film world as head of the Australian Film Commission in London, and for various executive roles at United Artists and Hoyts.

BC: When did you lose your Sundance virginity, and what were your first impressions of the festival?

GH: The first festival I did was 1994. It's changed a lot since those days... I think '94 was one of the last Sundances that was on a much smaller basis before it became a bigger international event. It was still important back then in terms of discovering new talent, but I definitely felt the change between my first visit in 1994 and the next one in 1996 with a movie called Blackrock. That was the year of Shine, and although I wasn't involved with that particularly movie, I think it kind of changed the shape of Sundance for international films.

BC: Could you provide a bit of background on how a sales agent works with a filmmaker at a festival like Sundance?

GH: The most important thing is to get all of the right decision makers into the screening. There's no better way of hyping a movie than getting all the competitors in one room, but that's a hard thing for a filmmaker to do on their own. For us, there's normally no problem getting these guys to show up for premieres, but if a film has already been seen at other festivals or markets prior to Sundance, then it's much harder to get the decision makers to come. There are of course exceptions to this... one example of an Australian movie, but again, a movie we weren't involved with, was The Castle. The film had extraordinary success at Sundance even though it had already been exposed at a couple of markets. I think that post The Castle, it became easier if there was a bit of buzz around a movie — decision makers would go back and see it with an audience. Before The Castle, that didn't tend to happen. I think that movie changed people's attitudes to watching films which had already been seen at other markets.

BC: If you were going to take a film to Sundance, how far ahead would you normally start preparing?

GH: Pretty much as soon as you know the film is in the festival. Of course, you can lobby Sundance all you like in terms of trying to push films that you think are right for them, but that doesn't necessary lead anywhere. I've had movies go to Sundance which I didn't expect to get in, and other movies which I thought were their sort of movies that just didn't get selected.

BC: How does a typical day tend to pan out for you in Park City during the festival?

GH: Well, I'm also there as a buyer, so my time is split between the sales activities on movies we're representing and buying films. I've bought a range of different movies at Sundance, both international rights to films and sometimes just the Australian rights. The main focus for Arclight now is worldwide rights to films, but I'm finding that as our company grows, we're less interested in films that premiere at a festival or market. In most cases, we like to be involved much earlier than this. Most decent movies are picked up immediately at Sundance, if not before, and if the movie doesn't perform at the festival, it's unlikely that anything great will happen to it afterward. That's not to say it's impossible, but a big U.S. deal is probably either going to happen at Sundance, or it will start being negotiated there and will be completed a couple of weeks later.

BC: Assuming you had formed a relationship with a producer, and you were going to take their film to Sundance as a sales agent, what sort of materials would you expect them to have produced for you?

GH: For Sundance... nothing really. I don't even think it's necessary to have a poster. I think campaigns which are too glossy often don't perform well at Sundance. It's kind of the opposite to Cannes, where you have to take heavy advertising in the trades, you've got to tell everyone about the movie, and so on. I don't think any of that's necessary at

Sundance. It's all about creating a hype of interest in seeing the movie amongst the seven or eight major acquisitions people there, and getting them to the screening. You definitely don't need to have posters all over Main Street or get big ads in *Variety* to make that happen.

BC: Is it common for sales agents to listen to pitches from producers at Sundance, either for completed films or projects in development?

GH: They do, but that's not really an important part of Sundance, to be honest.

BC: Sundance is known as a very American festival. How important is it for international films?

GH: I think it's quite important, particularly now that the World Cinema section has an award attached to it. There are a lot of international films that have been discovered and got major deals at Sundance, films like *Shine* and *The Castle* out of Australia and U.K. movies like *Saving Grace*. Those are just a couple that come to mind, but I'm sure there are many other examples, too.

BC: How much attention do you think the industry pays to the alternative festivals that take place in Park City during Sundance?

GH: Not a lot. I've been going to Sundance every year since 1996, and I think I've only been to Slamdance once. I don't think it's very important — the main focus is on the major part of the festival.

BC: Do you have any memorable Sundance anecdotes?

GH: Nothing specific comes to mind. I've had a lot of interesting experiences with a number of movies there over the years, but it wasn't that I walked away with a $10 million deal from a U.S. major or anything like that. I've had the experience of both premiering movies there and feeling quite disappointed by the reaction, and also showing films like *Bollywood Queen*, and a few years ago, *Forever Fever*, which were very much discovered at the festival, and the reaction was very positive.

BC: Are there any places where you find yourself socialising or networking more than others?

GH: I just go to screenings — that's what I do. When I'm not in meetings, I go to see films. Screenings are one of the most interesting experiences at Sundance. Looking back over many festivals, I think one thing about Sundance I would caution people about is the fact that the audience seems to react differently to films in Park City. Whether that's a combination of the altitude and the cold or just the excitement that's generated by the filmmakers having a lot of their own people in the screening, I don't know. I've seen films, such as *Girlfight* or *Happy, Texas*, for example, which I thought were extraordinary experiences the first time I saw them at Sundance, but on subsequent viewing couldn't really understand why I'd had that reaction in Park City.

BC: Do you have any general advice for future Sundance virgins, particularly filmmakers?

GH: I really think it's a good idea to get a sales agent involved early because, unless you have major cast attached, your film is in real danger of getting lost there. A lot of people go to Sundance looking for sales agents, but I think it's essential to have one much earlier than that. I can think of a couple of movies this year that I would have been interested in picking up before Sundance, but the minute Sundance was over, I wouldn't touch them.

Eugene Hernandez
Editor-in-Chief
indieWIRE (New York)

As the Editor-in-Chief of *indieWIRE*, Eugene Hernandez oversees all of the company's publications. In 1996, he co-founded the company, and the previous year, he co-founded *iLINE*, an online community for filmmakers that was the predecessor to *indieWIRE*. Eugene has participated as a juror and panelist at film festivals worldwide, including the Sundance Film Festival, the San Francisco International Film Festival, and the Tribeca Film Festival, as well as many others. He has contributed to *FILMMAKER* magazine, *Daily Variety*, *The Hollywood Reporter*, *Independent Film & Video Monthly*, and *RES* magazine and has served as a consultant to the Association of Independent Video and Filmmakers (AIVF) and the Creative Capital Foundation and as a funding panelist for the NEA and the Independent Television Service (ITVS). He is also a regular member of selection committees for the annual IFP/West Independent Spirit Awards.

Eugene spent five years at ABC-TV, ultimately working in its emerging multimedia division as a producer of Web sites for ABC News and the annual Academy Awards. While at UCLA, he headed the Campus Events Commission, overseeing a film program, lecture series, and concert promotion.

BC: When did you lose your Sundance virginity, and what were your first impressions of the festival?

EH: I went to Sundance for the first time in 1993, mostly in a non-professional way. At the time, I had just graduated from UCLA and was working in Los Angeles. While I was at school, I'd been involved in film screenings and programming, so I'd heard of the festival by way of seeing a number of Sundance films that had been shown at UCLA and thought it sounded interesting. Although I was working in Hollywood, I wasn't very satisfied with the direction my early career was taking, so a friend of mine and I decided just to go see what the festival was like. We'd each signed up for a package, but about a week before the festival, I ended up contacting Chris Gore at *Film Threat*, and he actually asked me to write something about the festival for that year. So while I didn't intend to go there in a professional capacity or as a journalist (at that stage I'd never written anything as a journalist before), I was able to secure a press accreditation as a freelancer for *Film Threat*. It was also a lot easier back then as there were far fewer journalists than there are now. I had originally intended to stay for just the first half of the festival but ended up having a really great time, and I met a load of terrific people, so I decided to extend my stay through to the end.

My first year at Sundance was really eye opening because it was my first time attending a festival of any kind. Sundance in the early '90s was clearly a different event from what it has become today. It was much smaller and more intimate, and going there as someone who was still trying to figure out which direction to go with their career was a really eye-opening thing because I met so many terrific people, people whom I'm still friends with today. For example, I met Mark Rabinowitz, who would go on to be one of the cofounders of indieWIRE with me. It was also the year of the "20-something filmmaker," so I met Robert Rodriguez and became acquainted with him; I met Bryan Singer and got to know him a bit better by hanging out with him back in Los Angeles; and a lot of other people around my own age, who were just getting involved with the independent film community at the time.

So it was a really terrific experience all round, and I remember being struck by the fact that at a film festival, you could not only see all of these films for the first time but also meet the filmmakers and talk to them about their films. I remember thinking, "This is really a special opportunity." Since then, I've gone to the festival every year minus one, but that first time at Sundance, I was not only a Sundance virgin but a film-festival virgin as well, so the whole thing was a very exciting experience.

BC: What about Park City itself? What were your first impressions of the town?

EH: Well, to be honest, the experience was a bit jarring. Because I'd grown up in Southern California and lived there back then (I now live in New York), I'd never really spent any time in snow or cold weather of any sort. Arriving in Salt Lake City and seeing all the snow on the ground and then getting the ride to Park City were not only shocking because of the altitude, but also because it was the first time I'd been in weather that cold for an extended period of time. I adjusted pretty quickly, but initially that was a bit of an experience as well.

BC: These days in your capacity as Editor-in-Chief of indieWIRE, what sort of preparation do you do ahead of Sundance?

EH: Our preparation actually starts months in advance. In September, we're already planning for our coverage of the festival in January, and it normally starts with some of the logistics of covering the event. We bring a team of people to Sundance every year, so we start making logistical plans, start working out our budget, where we're going to stay, when we're going to work, and so on. Then, as the festival gets closer, particularly after the October submission deadline passes, we begin to hear about some of the films that will be playing at the festival. At that point, we start tracking those films to make sure that when the festival does roll around in January, our coverage is as informed as possible.

So even in October, we're talking with filmmakers who have projects that will go, we're thinking about ways we might cover the festival, and we're looking at the films we might want to highlight in the early days of the event. Once November rolls around, that's when it starts getting busier in terms of the advance word on films that will be selected, so we start to get a better sense of what the line-up will look like. Then, in late November or early December, the Sundance organisers announce the films for the main sections of the festival. At that point, most of our attention is focused on trying to get as much information as possible about those films, so December is normally almost as busy as our coverage during the festival itself. We're talking to filmmakers, we're talking to publicists, and it tends to be a lot of long days and nights just trying to get all of our ducks in a row. So planning begins in September and gets a lot more intense as the festival gets closer.

BC: How does a typical day tend to pan out for you in Park City during the festival?

EH: A typical day at Sundance... it's funny because in some ways, Sundance just feels like one long day to me. We try to get there on the Tuesday before the festival starts, and we stay until the Monday after it ends. So we spend just under two weeks in Park City. It ends up feeling like one day that doesn't really end... one long, two-week day.

But seriously, on a typical day once the festival begins, I try to get up early — and sometimes that can be hard, depending on how late you were out the night before — and around 8:30 or 9:00, I usually start by just making

sure everything's in shape in terms of our coverage. That's both what we've posted overnight and working with our Web folks, who are based off-site at GMD Studios in Florida. I also usually try to check out some of the other publications and see what they're writing about that day, see how it complements or is consistent (or not) with what we're doing. I try to read the local papers and any other places that have festival coverage also, to get a sense of what people are talking about outside of the festival.

Invariably, there's a lot of information that's constantly going back and forth, and as the day starts, we begin to hear about films that screened well the night before, or we talk with some of the reps or people involved with the films and find out a bit about what's happening that day. We're also going through the photos from the night before to see what we might want to run in indieWIRE — we do a printed publication during the festival that comes out every day, so a good deal of the morning is spent looking at yesterday's photos and working with writers to fine-tune any articles that are more feature driven. There's also another aspect to this which is the distribution of the print publication. This happens before noon, and we have to manage the people who help us distribute the publication, making sure it gets out to the right places.

On top of all this, the goal for me is always to try and see at least one or two films per day. I don't get to see as many films as I would like at Sundance, simply because we have so many things going on, and as the editor of the publication, I have a lot of responsibilities. But I do try to see at least one film a day, sometimes two. It's usually one in the morning and then one earlier in the afternoon before our deadline starts to loom later in the day.

Because Sundance is a place that draws so many different people, there are also invariably any number of meetings that I have to try and fit in amongst seeing films and working on the publications. And on top of that, there are any number of receptions and parties on any given day. We try to have someone at just about every single official and unofficial event that takes place at the festival, either one of our editors or freelance writers. We consider the festival extremely important because it's a launching pad for specialty films and for emerging filmmakers, so we try to cover it as aggressively as possible because we believe it sets the tone for the rest of the year.

BC: What's the craziest thing a filmmaker did to try and attract your attention as a journalist?

EH: The funniest thing that's happened to me in a while at Sundance happened in 2003. It was the middle of the week, and it was getting late in the day — I think it was maybe 6:00 pm or 7:00 pm, or something like that. Our deadline for the print publication is usually early evening, so we were rushing to try and finish everything — it was one of those days where everything was happening at once, and it was extremely busy. We hadn't had time to eat, and everybody was starving, but we also had another event at 8:00 pm. We still had to drop the materials off to Copy Depot, where we print the publication, so we were trying to figure out how we could manage to eat something before the next engagement. Suddenly, there's a knock on the door, and there's this delivery guy holding a pizza. We all kind of looked at each other to try and figure out who ordered it, but no one did. The delivery guy says, "Are you Eugene Hernandez from *indieWIRE*?" I said, "Yes." And he said, "Well, this is for you." So I accepted the delivery and opened up the pizza-box. Inside, pasted on the lid, there's a flyer for a film as well as a steaming hot pizza — clearly we couldn't have been happier to have a pizza arrive at that moment. It turned out that the flyer was for a film playing in one of the alternative festivals, and I trusted the safety of the pizza because it was actually a promotion for a film by a couple of guys I'd met on my first trip to Sundance 10 years before. I hadn't talked to them or seen them in 10 years, so I guess they somehow heard about indieWIRE, remembered my name, and decided to send over some food for us at dinnertime. It was greatly appreciated.

BC: That's a wonderful story. Do you have any other anecdotes you like to recount when the topic of Sundance comes up?

EH: I think my most memorable experiences were during the whole era in the late '90s, around '99 and 2000. I had the most unique experiences during that time because of the influx of people and cash that came from the whole dotcom explosion. There were so many people, so much money being spent, and the parties people were having were just so extravagant. I think the late '90s were really a turning point for the festival; even though Sundance kind of exploded in the early '90s as a showcase for films, it exploded as a destination in the late '90s. That was a really interesting time. Just being there and seeing the incredible interest people had in the festival as a place, not just as a film festival but as a destination — a winter opportunity to promote yourself, your film, and your company. It still happens a great deal now, but in a different way.

Equally interesting and a load of fun was the year of Slumdance in 1997. That was one of the most unique experiences I've ever had at Sundance. They took over the old Mrs. Fields cookie factory on Main Street and created a late-night hangout, not only for seeing films, but also for just getting away from it all. They had DJs and performers, and it drew a lot of people, not only festivalgoers, but celebrities as well. I remember seeing John Waters down there one day, and Tim Robbins another. It was probably one of the most fun couple of nights I've every had at Sundance simply because it was not just about the films, but also about meeting new people and hanging out in a cool, fun environment. And I also got, I think, one of the worst flus I've ever had at Sundance that year. It kind of ruined the final weekend, but that's another thing that tends to happen when you're there working very hard.

BC: I guess your body was punishing you for all the fun you'd been having.

EH: [laughs] Yeah. As I've gotten older, I've learned how to better pace myself — you don't necessarily have to go out every night until 2:00 am or 3:00 am. You can pace yourself, but I like to say, "It's a marathon, not a sprint."

BC: Do you have any favourite places to eat in Park City?

EH: Sure, a few. I think it's always important to stay nourished, but it can be hard to do that amongst the craziness of a festival. Sometimes my favourite place to eat is a nice restaurant when it's a party hosted by a company, when someone else is paying the bill — we run a very low-budget operation in Park City. We also try to at least once or twice during the festival get some people together and go out for a dinner where you can sit down and have a decent meal and some nice conversation. There's a terrific Spanish restaurant at the bottom of Main Street called Picasso — we had a nice party there one year — and Zoom has some great food — there's always a party there. I also like the breakfast at The Eating Establishment if I have a little more time; otherwise, it's often a quick egg sandwich from the Main Street Deli. But to be honest, I usually don't have a lot of time to do too many full sit-down meals. Because we stay in a condo, we have a full kitchen, so often we just go to the grocery store, and someone will make something in the morning or the evening, and we'll simply eat at home.

BC: What about networking or socialising — I guess for you it's more about networking? Are there any venues you prefer more than others?

EH: Well, it's pretty easy to network at Sundance because of the number of people that come to the festival and the fact that they really take over the town. You can go just about anywhere and run into someone who's there for Sundance or Slamdance, or whatever. Clearly there are also any number of parties that are taking place, either official parties or unofficial parties, although the hard part is of course getting in.

I was always disappointed when the official parties that Sundance presents lost favour, although I think they've regained favour a little bit over recent years. In the early '90s, when I first went to Sundance, the official party was the place that everyone went to start their evening. It kicked off around 9:00 pm, and you would literally see everybody who was there for the festival. Then at that party, you would start to hear about the after-parties at so-and-so's condo. You would all head on up to the house, and you were able to develop these bonds and friendships with people because you'd see the same people every night. As the festival grew, a lot of the companies started hosting private parties that competed with the official parties. It started segmenting the audience, so there were a few years where the official parties were very quiet. But I always thought that the official parties were great because there were still a lot of people, especially emerging filmmakers who didn't get invited to the big elite parties. Often they are the most interesting people to talk to. And to be honest, these days there are so many elite parties going on, and getting into them can be a real chore. It normally involves standing in line for half an hour, and once you're inside, they are so crowded that you can't move. Everybody's fighting to get into this one party, and once you're inside, you realise that you don't want to be there anyway.

Some of the best nights I've had in recent years have been at smaller parties in people's condos. A friend of mine threw one a couple of years ago, and it was just really nice. It had maybe 40 or 50 people there, a good mix of industry and filmmakers, and was just really comfortable. Those are the best places, not only for networking, but for forging more solid relationships with people whom you will stay in touch with after the festival. At these big, more-exclusive parties, it's just so much harder to do that.

BC: Do you have any general advice for future Sundance virgins?

EH: I guess a big piece of advice would be, "Don't believe the hype." I think it's very easy to buy into that Sundance "overnight success" hype, but the reality is that even people who get written about as these overnight successes have spent years getting to that point. And there's countless examples of films that got picked up for a lot of money at Sundance and went absolutely nowhere later in the year. So I think it's important, not just for filmmakers but for anybody going to Sundance, to be critical in a certain respect of the attention that the festival gets. Sundance is a terrific festival — the folks who run it are really talented, and they do care — but it's just very easy for people who go there and get too focused on the industry aspects of the event and in the process and kind of lose sight of the opportunities you have at a festival like Sundance.

So when I'm there, I always try to remember that very first year I went and the terrific experience I had when I didn't really know anybody, and I was just there to meet people and see movies. That's what I love about Sundance, and it's still there. With all the TV coverage of "celebrities in the snow," it's very easy to forget the festival is about movies and about filmmakers. Even though some films now have celebrities in them, there is still a wonderful range of films presented... short films, documentaries. The World Cinema section, both for documentary and narrative, is also a rare opportunity to see a lot of these films on the big screen. The festival is really about discovery, and I know it's a term that gets criticised at times, but for me it is about discovery; it's about seeing films from filmmakers whom I'm learning about for the very first time. And it happens every year... every year I find a filmmaker or a film, typically more than one, that just excites me, energises me, and makes me glad that I'm doing what I do. Sometimes you have to dig a little bit deeper to find these films, but they're always there, and that's why I like the festival so much.

Andrew Herwitz
President
The Film Sales Company (New York)

The Film Sales Company is a New York–based domestic sales agent/producer's rep. The company specializes in securing domestic distribution for English and foreign-language finished films (both fiction and documentary) as well as financing for English-language packaged projects. Prior to establishing this company, Andrew was at Miramax for six years, most recently as co-head of the film acquisitions department. He is a graduate of Harvard University, Columbia Business School, and Harvard Law School.

BC: When did you lose your Sundance virginity, and what were your first impressions of Park City and the festival itself?

AH: My first trip to Sundance was about seven years ago while I worked at Miramax. My entire impression of the event was formed driving be-

tween the Stein Eriksen Lodge, where we did deals in Harvey Weinstein's suite, and the various screening rooms around Sundance, where we watched films. I'd say it was a real trial by fire. We bought four films in five days, so I didn't get to see a lot of daylight. I saw none of the city, I only got to eat when someone brought me food, my eyes were only open at night or in the darkness of a screening, and I don't think I even went to any parties. I never used my ski boots and have never brought any ski equipment to Park City again.

BC: Could you provide a bit of background on the role of a sales agent in relation to a festival like Sundance?

AH: Once a film has been accepted into a festival, it's in the schedule, and it's in the catalogue, but aside from a handful of distribution companies which can afford to bring a large team to a festival, most companies just don't have the resources to cover every single film playing at an event. So the sales agent performs several functions. First of all, they alert the various distributors to a film's existence, and if you're a sales agent with some degree of credibility, you can help steer the appropriate distributor to a screening of your film. Second, once you're in discussions with a distributor, you have the opportunity to whet their appetite with marketing suggestions or angles that they perhaps haven't thought of... basically, you try to give them greater incentive to want to buy the film and/or help them have ammunition to excite their colleagues and, more importantly, their bosses. Third, it's about negotiating the best deal for the film, including possibly trying to spark a bidding war amongst rival distributors to help bolster the price. Finally, of course, it's about closing the deal, making sure that the distributor does not leave the room until the deal has been signed and the rights to the film have been sold. Historically, the films that sell for the greatest amounts of money are always represented by some kind of sales agent.

BC: So you would say that having professional representation is pretty important for someone looking to sell their film at an event like Sundance?

AH: I think it's essential. Most filmmakers don't have the relationships to ensure that the distributor is at the screening. Even if the distributor is there, and even if they are interested in the film, without the participation of a sales agent, I think it's extremely difficult for a producer and/or director to negotiate on their own effectively. It's much easier to have an intermediary who's as anxious for the film to be sold as the filmmakers, but who's also perhaps less emotionally involved and can therefore bring a degree of objectivity to the negotiation.

BC: If you were taking a film to Sundance, what sort of preparation would you do ahead of the festival, and how far ahead would you start planning?

AH: The first step of course is to become familiar with the film and the filmographies of everyone involved, particularly the director and the cast. Then you see which other companies may have previously distributed films produced and/or directed by that team, and certainly any companies that have upcoming films with members of the cast in them. You really want to focus on those companies because they already have a vested interest in the particular actor or actress, and once they've started to spend money and time to promote the career of one individual, they will often be more inclined to handle the next film with that actor or actress to help protect their investment.

Sometime between late December and early January, you start calling the various distributors to let them know you're handling the film and give them a taste of what it's about. You start helping them form a concept in their mind about the story line and atmosphere of the film, without giving away too much and raising expectations too high. You do want positive expectations definitely, but you don't want to over-hype them because if you do that, the distributors will invariably be disappointed when they see the film.

BC: So once you're in Park City for the festival, how does a typical day tend to pan out for you?

AH: Various sales agents work in different ways, but for me, I have a lean team on the ground in Park City. I personally go to each screening of every film I'm representing. A lot of my time is taken up with these screenings, meeting with interested distributors, and talking about those films. My day also often involves meetings with other people in the industry to talk business or generally schmooze. And then there are people I'm genuinely friendly with whom I'll always have a meal with or pal around with at every festival or market we attend. I also try to go and see other movies that are screening during the festival, either movies that seem not to have representation or movies that I just want to see. Sadly, there usually isn't as much time for the latter as I would like.

BC: If you are going to take a film to Sundance, what sort of materials would you expect the producer to provide for you to support the sales efforts?

AH: I don't think they need to have explicit marketing materials or anything like that. The film really speaks for itself, so I think it's the relationship that I as a sales agent have with the distributor that gets them to the screening, not a flyer or a poster, although these things don't hurt.

BC: At Sundance, is it common for sales agents to hear pitches or meet with producers who are seeking representation for their films?

AH: That may happen, but a sales agent typically would want to see the film before they sign on to represent it. Given the hectic pace of the schedule at Sundance, there's not a lot of time to sit and screen films which are unrelated to the festival. Usually what happens is you may meet with a producer whose film you've been tracking and set up some other time to screen it.

BC: How much attention does the industry, specifically distributors, pay to the alternative festivals that take place in Park City alongside Sundance?

AH: I represented a film that won Slamdance in 2002. I think if a film

wins something in one of these events, that definitely gets attention. But I still think you need a good advocate to make sure the distributors come and see your film, more so if it's screening in one of these events.

BC: Do you have any favourite places to eat when you're in Park City?

AH: There was a pleasant little café by the Marriott Summit Watch which I used to go to a lot, but that's closed now. I quite like the cyber café [Alpine Internet Coffeehouse], which is also down near the Summit Watch.

BC: What about when it's time to kick back? Do you have any places you like for socialising or networking?

AH: When it's time to kick back, I go back to my hotel to sleep.

BC: Do you have any advice for future Sundance virgins, particularly filmmakers?

AH: Don't park in the Albertsons car park — you *will* be towed. But seriously, I think it's a good opportunity to meet people, but don't expect anyone will have time to screen your film during the festival.

Charlotte Mickie

Managing Director,
Celluloid Dreams
(Canada)

Charlotte Mickie is Managing Director of French sales company Celluloid Dreams. Previously, Mickie headed up international motion picture sales, at Alliance Atlantis Entertainment Group. In this role, Charlotte oversaw all aspects of motion-picture acquisitions, presales, and sales for the company's Entertainment Group. She has acted as the international theatrical sales agent for a wide variety of successful independent films, including Tom McCarthy's *The Station Agent*, David Gordon Green's *All the Real Girls*, Michael Moore's *Bowling for Columbine*, Atom Egoyan's *The Sweet Hereafter*, Todd Solondz's *Welcome to the Dollhouse*, Greg Mottola's *The Daytrippers*, and Neil LaBute's *In the Company of Men*.

Charlotte is an Executive Board member of the American Film Marketing Association (AFMA) and serves on the board of The Power Plant, a major, non-collecting, contemporary, public art gallery. She is also on the Advisory Board for Rogers Industry Center at the Toronto International Film Festival. Charlotte studied English literature and art history as an undergraduate in the Joint Honours program at McGill University.

BC: When did you lose your Sundance virginity, and what were your first impressions of the festival?

CM: The first time I was there, we were selling *Twist*, which was about 11 or 12 years ago. The festival was already becoming quite famous at that point and had grown beyond being a small insider thing where people mainly went to ski. I think the initial idea behind the festival was that they would show these independent movies and lure people from the studios there who wanted to do the skiing; maybe they'd catch a few films, and a bit of business would be done on the slopes. By the time I started going to the festival, people might have taken an afternoon off to ski, but basically they were there to scout and buy films.

BC: And what about Park City? How did you find the town itself?

CM: Well, first of all, it seemed dreadfully difficult to get to. There were no direct flights to Salt Lake City from Canada, so you always had to transfer through Chicago or one of the other hubs, and then there's the long drive in a shuttle bus to Park City itself.

I don't think I'd been to the mountains in B.C. or Alberta at that point, so it was really the first time I had seen the Rockies. I was surprised by how remote and wistful it was, how quickly it became dark, and how dark it got. If you've been living in a big urban centre, there's quite a difference between being in a place that's that remote and being in a place where the sky is grey, even at night.

And then, of course, there were the challenges of the town itself because it's relatively spread out. They do have shuttle buses, but that was a challenge back then, and the accommodations at that point were also very much for people who came for ski trips. They weren't suited to business travellers at all. A lot of the hotels had very thin walls and barely adequate heating. I was always cold at night, and it was very uncomfortable. The festival is still pretty spread out these days, and that's one of the challenges. It can be difficult to get from screening to screening if you don't have a car, and even if you do, the traffic is now incredibly jammed, which can also be frustrating.

But I do think the way that Park City has developed around the festival is a really good thing, though. I mean the accommodations are much better now, there's more choice, and the addition of venues like the Eccles has been nothing but a good thing. It was nice when it was small, but there is still an intimacy to it, certainly from a business perspective. I also think that the people in Park City are much more adjusted to us coming and being there. They tend to see us more as generating income for the town now, as opposed to just seeing us as weirdoes who they should be hostile to because we take their parking spaces.

BC: Could you provide a bit of background on the role of a sales agent, particularly in relation to a festival like Sundance?

CM: Sundance is peculiar in a good and bad way for us. On the plus side, it's one of the few festivals where there are a fairly healthy number of movies that are unspoken for, in other words, movies that don't have American distribution or an international sales agent. The other positive thing is that there are a certain number of very elite international territorial buyers who attend and are prepared to give me a read on what they think of the movies. The bad part of Sundance is that most of the films are angling for American distribution, and if possible, a world deal with one of the classics divisions of the major studios. So they tend to think about U.S. distribution or a world deal before they think about an international sales agent.

But that aside, I think there's a fun aspect to it as well because there is a fairly collegial feeling amongst the American distributors. Even though they are ultimately competitors and they sometimes go after the same films, they're not cutthroat competitors. I guess there's a kind of hope at a festival like Sundance that each company will find the right film for them, and that they won't necessarily all be going after the same things. These guys, they all know each other, and they're all friends, so they kind of sit together at the back of the Eccles Theater with some of the buyers and quite a few of the sales agents. We end up in this little coterie in the back rows, actually having a bit of fun together watching the films.

BC: Sundance is known as a very American festival. How important is it for international films, and is there much acquisitions activity from foreign buyers?

CM: I think there's a resistance from foreign buyers to buying directly from the producers, and the producer's reps tend not to be that keen on doing territorial sales at Sundance. There is some buying that takes place territorially at the festival, but a lot of the buyers hold back for sales agents to come on board. But it does happen. This year [2003], I think *Girls Will Be Girls* got sold to Japan directly, and when Miramax bought *The Station Agent*, they also bought Italy. I think the main problem is that the foreign films at the festival do take a bit of a second place to the American movies, particularly movies in competition. I know Sundance is working on changing this, and I think these films are really enjoyed by the general public at the festival, but in terms of attention from buyers, they really take second place at the moment.

BC: Perhaps part of that has to do with the fact that a lot of the World Cinema program, particularly the dramatic features, tend to have already played one or two festivals before they get to Sundance?

CM: There is that, but there are also occasionally premieres of non-American movies. Shine was a huge

thing at Sundance, and the Irish film *Bloody Sunday* did really well last year. *The War Zone* — the Tim Roth film he directed about child abuse — also premiered at the festival and did quite well. So there are exceptions both to the success rate and the premiere thing you mentioned, but there's probably a way of making it work better. I think both Sundance and the sales agents are working on that, but part of the problem is that for independent distribution companies and classics divisions, it's possible to create a buzz in the States about buying an American film at Sundance — there's publicity value in getting into a bidding war with Harvey [Weinstein]. For international distributors, that's just not the case.

BC: These days, if you were taking films to Sundance or working with films in the official program, what sort of preparation would you do ahead of the festival, and how far ahead would you start?

CM: Well, I would certainly get in touch with all of my buyers to let them know that they can see the film at Sundance, but I don't know if I would do trade advertising or anything like that. We'd also try to arrange to bring the actors and director to Sundance, and maybe see if we could get some postering done. I had *Twist* there many years ago, and that was an interesting case because the film had already been in the Toronto International Film Festival, so it certainly had exposure, and we'd actually already sold the television rights to Disney. To promote the film, I put on a party in this place on Main Street called 'Z' Place — it's called something else now — which was a kind of auditorium with a stage and a big hall. To support the film, I brought Hank Ballard to Park City for Sundance. Hank is the African American singer who originally wrote and performed "The Twist," which Chubby Checker later covered. Chubby's version is the one that made all the money and became famous, but it's virtually identical to Hank's version. Hank was quite senior, although perpetually young, and he brought his band. I put on a dinner for the film at 'Z' Place, and Hank and the band performed, and they just went nuts. People had an absolutely fantastic time. Hank passed away in 2003 — in retrospect, I wish we'd filmed it because I think it was an event of archival importance. In any case, as a result of seeing the film and their experience at the party, New Line bought the video rights for Twist.

BC: How does a typical day in Park City tend to pan out for you during the festival?

CM: It really depends on what my focus is that year. One year, I think I had seven films in the festival, so I just spent all of my time running between screenings of my films and taking buyer attendance. It got so bad that I actually walked into one cinema, wrote down all of the buyers, and then suddenly realised it wasn't even my film! Last year [2003], my sales slate was pretty light, so all I did was go to screenings. I would see about four or five films a day. I'd start with the 9:00 am screening at the Eccles, go to the next one at the Library; then in the afternoon, I'd try to see one at 4:00 pm and one in the evening at 9:00 pm. I must say I hate the midnight screenings — they're just a bit too much. Last year, one of the problems I had was trying to fit everything in. I mean, when the Cannes Film Festival is on, our world shuts down, but Sundance is not quite the same thing. It's a very important event, but business tends to go on, so I spent a lot of time trying to do my regular work as well as being at Sundance.

We do try to go out for dinner now and then, although often it tends to be squeezing it in. I think the whole approach of the restaurants is misguided — this idea of having elaborate six-course sit-down meals. This might be okay after a long day's skiing, but if you're in town for Sundance, you just don't have time for it. I realise that their goal is to make as much money as they possibly can during Sundance, but I think they could make just as much money using a "rapid turnover" approach.

BC: Assuming you'd formed a relationship with a producer, and you were going to rep their film at Sundance, what sort of materials would you have expected them to have produced for you?

CM: I don't expect the producers to come up with anything in terms of sales materials, frankly. We do a lot of that ourselves, or we do it in conjunction with the American distributor. Sundance is not a place where you show people the trailer for the movie. I think one film that was really a triumph of marketing at Sundance was The Blair Witch Project, but that was because the marketing was Internet focused — a new thing at the time. I think that was very persuasive in terms of getting people to the screenings, and persuasive in Artisan's purchase of the film. But I don't think it's been repeated since.

BC: Yeah, that's the example that people tend to hold up as Sundance "marketing glory," but it's the exception rather than the rule.

CM: Definitely. To the extent that there's business going on at the festival, it's on a wholesale level; it's insiders. These people don't tend to be won over by clever marketing that producers come up with, simply because these people are marketers themselves.

BC: Is it common for sales agents to listen to pitches from producers at Sundance?

CM: It happens, and I think that there is a fair amount of it. I personally find it difficult to focus on listening to pitches when I'm there, but I'll definitely take one.

BC: How much attention do you think the industry pays to the alternative events that take place in Park City alongside Sundance?

CM: I think everybody kind of watches them out of the corner of their eye because something could sneak up and surprise you. There have been a couple of things out of Slamdance that I've worked on... The Daytrippers, and this year, a film called Milwaukee, Minnesota, which went on to the Critics' Week at Cannes. In fact, the Critics' Week kind of takes pride in finding things that Sundance didn't take and turning them into little

hits. The Daytrippers, in terms of sales, also performed really well.

BC: Do you have a memorable anecdote from your many trips to Sundance that you like to recount?

CM: There are probably a lot of funny stories — I'm sure I've forgotten most of them — but there are a couple that stand out for me. One was the year that Shine played. When I walked into the screening room, there were a lot of American and territorial distributors that I recognised... I walked in a bit late, but it was so clearly a buzz event. I think maybe I'd missed a market before or something or that people just weren't expecting to see me, but everyone turned around and said, "Hello, Charlotte." It was really nice, and I felt like I had all these friends — it was a wonderful professional moment. And the atmosphere at the end of that screening was just amazing. This business is tough, and it can make people feel very negative toward films, but the number of really cranky, jaded, touchy people who were in tears at the end of that screening was just breathtaking. You knew there were going to be fistfights over this movie. It wasn't my movie, but I was very affected by it because when a movie really does work in that way on a wholesale level, it's very exciting.

Another anecdote I guess would be the year of In the Company of Men. We had the international sales rights for the film, but for a number of reasons, we decided not to disclose this during Sundance. It didn't have much buzz going into the festival, and the first screening was almost a non-event. But enough people were outraged, so the film did start to generate a buzz after that, and by the time we got to the last screening, the cinema was packed. Even though we had the rights, I went to the screening to encourage people to believe that we didn't have them, and ended up having to lie on the floor during the screening because there was no space left. Anyone who has seen the movie knows it can seem quite vicious, and this was particularly acute then, when there was no context — people in the screening were just taking these deep breaths. But as it went on, they started to get that it was funny and that it was actually really cruel to the men in the movie, rather than women in general. So there was this sort of simultaneous horror and laughter — it was just an electric atmosphere.

After the screening, I got pulled aside by a PR woman who was furious. She was just like, "I can't believe that movie. It is the most awful movie I have EVER seen!" And she was furious with ME, perhaps just because I was the closest person at the time. That was a bit nerve racking. In saying that, it was interesting to see how the perception of the movie changed over time. Initially everyone hated the film, and no one wanted to buy it. But as a result of people debating it, reviews coming out, and ultimately it being in the Directors' Fortnight at Cannes, it sold through the roof in most territories. That was just very interesting.

BC: Do you have any favourite places to eat when you're in Park City?

CM: I kind of like Blind Dog Grill, which is a new restaurant down in Prospector Square. I think the food is... and maybe the restaurateurs will forgive me for my previous comments if I say this... I think the food in Park City is really good everywhere. It might be a little elaborate for the time constraints, but it is good.

BC: What about when it comes to networking or socialising? Are there any venues you tend to find yourself in more than others?

CM: You can still bump into a lot of people at the Yarrow, but I'm not sure why that's the case. But you know, even though Park City is spread out, it's still pretty small, so you're always bumping into people pretty much wherever you go.

BC: Do you have any general advice for future Sundance virgins?

CM: If you don't know how to drive, take driving lessons. But seriously, it's quite a vibrant atmosphere, so I think people get it pretty fast. The altitude buzz doesn't hurt either.

Mark Pogachefsky
Co-President
mPRm (Los Angeles)

Mark Pogachefsky is co-president of mPRm, a public relations agency specializing in entertainment, new media, and communications companies and their products. He was founder and president of The Pogachefsky Company, established in January 1992, which merged with Rachel McCallister and Associates and KillerAppCommunications in July 1998 to form mPRm.

Handling both production and release campaigns, the film division of mPRm currently represents or has represented such projects as *American Splendor, Swimming Pool, Wonderland, Elephant, Calendar Girls, Pieces of April, The Pianist, In the Bedroom, Traffic, You Can Count on Me, Memento,* and *LA Confidential.* mPRm represents films at international festivals, such as Sundance, Cannes, and Toronto, and corporate clients like Lion's Gate Releasing, Serendipity Point Films, the BAFTA Awards, and the Independent Spirit Awards.

Prior to opening his firm, Mark was a senior vice president at Andrea Jaffe and Associates and worked on *Bugsy, The Grifters,* and *Truth or Dare.* He began his publicity career in 1984 at Clein + Feldman, where he worked on film campaigns for *Kiss of the Spider Woman, The Trip to Bountiful, Mona Lisa, She's Gotta Have It, Heathers, Dirty Dancing, sex, lies and videotape, Drugstore Cowboy, Cinema Paradiso,* and *Steel Magnolias.*

Mark began his entertainment industry career in 1982 at Paramount Pictures as assistant editor of the *Paramount News,* the company's in-house magazine. Born and raised in Philadelphia, he is a graduate of Temple University.

BC: When did you lose your Sundance virginity, and what were your first impressions of the festival?

MP: The first time I went to the festival was in 1991. In many ways, it was quite different then... mainly much smaller than it is now. I went up there with a movie which was in one of the sidebar sections. I think it was possibly my first or second film festival ever — the festival was definitely smaller and more low key. In saying that, because I was staying in Deer Valley, I did feel very much on the periphery of the event and perhaps a little clueless about the whole thing.

BC: And how did you find Park City itself?

MP: Park City is a lovely little town, but it's grown quite a bit since my first trip. There's been a lot of development, particularly in terms of the number of condos, and back then almost everything was centred on Main Street. These days it's definitely more spread out, and there are more theatres and venues than there used to be. But on my first trip, I just remember it being a nice little quaint town.

BC: These days, what sort of preparation do you do ahead of your arrival in Park City for the festival?

MP: For us, it tends to work out in two ways. For movies that are in the Premiere section of the festival, these are often films that we're already representing, so we're able to start much earlier. For movies in the competitive and American Spectrum sections, we don't necessarily get involved until they're accepted into the festival in late November or early December.

The biggest thing pre-festival for us is making sure that people have their materials in hand. That includes press kits, production notes, stills, clips, if they're available, and so on. Then there's all the stuff around the movie — who's coming, how long are they staying, are we doing a dinner, are we doing a party, is there a sponsor, etc.? For movies we're working on with regular clients, there's a studio or distribution company involved to help with the preparation, but for other movies, we kind of become the de facto studio. We put together packets of information on each of the films we're working on and get these out to the press. If the movie's

for sale, we try to work with the sales agent on the acquisition strategy and decide whether we're going to show it to anybody ahead of time. And then there's a little thing called Christmas and New Year's that come in there as well. After the holidays, it's mostly about working on the finer details, like where we're going to do the interviews, what space we have, is the condo big enough, and when can we get out of there and come home... which invariably is the Sunday following the end of the festival.

BC: So once you're in Park City for the festival, how does a typical day tend to pan out for you?

MP: Generally, we would be at the festival with around 10–12 movies. That would be a combination of Premieres, that are generally studio related, a couple of movies in the Dramatic Competition, a couple in the Documentary Competition...it just depends on what the mix is that year. I'm normally up there with a staff of 10–12 people, so every movie has its own executive, and then there's also a backup person as well. Every morning, we have a meeting, and it's kind of really "divide and conquer": "You're going to the start of this screening; I'm going to the end of that screening; You're covering the interviews with these people; You'll be on Main Street." We basically go through it all and assign out the day, and then some days are easy, and some days are hard. The first half of the festival tends to be harder than the second. Friday, Saturday, Sunday, Monday, Tuesday...they're definitely harder than Wednesday, Thursday, and Friday. By the second half, the die have pretty much been cast, so you know if a movie you have is working... if you're begging people, or you're turning them away.

BC: How does a publicist typically work with an independent filmmaker leading up to a festival like Sundance?

MP: To put it bluntly, it's kind of, "Get your shit together." If a smart or savvy filmmaker has, in the process of making their film, also thought about the marketing and release of the film, then they'll have written production notes, will have stills, and that will make my job much easier. If not, then everything has to be done from scratch. The exact nature of these things is largely dependent on a) the film, b) the section it is in, and c) who stars in it. For example, being in World Cinema has a completely different set of requirements to being in the Dramatic Competition. Actually, World Cinema is in many ways one of the most interesting sections of the festival, but publicitywise it's also the hardest.

BC: Yeah. I guess with Sundance being the first festival of the year, there may not be a lot of information about foreign films coming in unless they've played at other festivals?

MP: Right. But also it's like, there are the Premieres, there are the dramas, there are the docs, there are American Spectrum, Midnight, Native Forum, Frontier... Most of the press that go are either going for the stars and premieres, or they're going for the dramas and docs. You can only see so many films in one day, so if I'm the guy in Dallas, and my paper

is sending me to Sundance, they're not sending me for World Cinema.

BC: Are there any general strategies that work well for raising awareness for a film in Park City during Sundance?

MP: The thing that I would say is that ultimately it is not about the interview schedule for the filmmakers; it's about who's seeing the movie, what their reaction is, and how we, in concert with the filmmakers' representatives, can use that to further the acquisition of the movie. At the end of the day, the buyer doesn't care if somebody's on *Entertainment Tonight* — they care what the New York Times thinks of the movie. So in a way, the strategy is to find the 10 people who you think will like the movie...understanding of course that that's an inexact science.

BC: Those people are distributors?

MP: No, I'm talking about press people. In other words, if we assume that the acquisitions people are going to see the movie because that's their job, then their first question is going to be, "What do the press think?" Because, of course, no one can make up their own mind. So what you have to be able to do as the publicist is use your knowledge of the press landscape and help direct the right press to the right movie.

BC: So a lot of your work is tailoring the message to the tastes of individual journalists?

MP: Inasmuch as one can, and understanding that there's no accounting for taste. There are certainly times where it's been like, "This person will love this movie," and they've hated the movie.

BC: How much attention does the industry pay to the alternative festivals that take place in Park City during Sundance?

MP: I think that outside of Slamdance, not much. I've never represented a film in any of those sub-festivals. It's like, if I've got 10 movies in Sundance, believe me, that's plenty. I think ultimately Slamdance will be the "Directors' Fortnight" of Sundance; I think it will evolve into the sort of "granddaddy of the sidebars" in the same way that the Directors' Fortnight has evolved at Cannes, where it's sort of separate but equal. But once you get below that, no. It would be pretty much impossible for me or my staff to get out of our Sundance hats to put on a Slamdance hat. It just wouldn't work.

BC: Do you have any favourite places to eat in Park City?

MP: Yeah, The Eating Establishment… breakfast at The Eating Establishment, the ribs at Zoom, and Grappa for the fancy überdinner. Those would be my choices.

BC: What about places to network or socialise? Are there any places in Park City which are better than others?

MP: For me, not really. Because I kind of get on a train in the morning, and I don't get off until the end of the day; it's often just the corner on Main Street where I happen to be standing at any given moment. In

saying that, I do like the lobby of the Eccles Theater — you can see a lot of people go by there.

BC: Do you have any advice for future Sundance virgins, particularly filmmakers?

MP: My main advice would be for somebody to actually take the time to make the best movie they can and not worry about festival deadlines or dates. If the movie isn't ready for Sundance, it isn't ready for Sundance. And that's okay. Sadly, and this is true of most festivals, the odds of acceptance are against you, so there isn't much point in making a substandard movie just to try and be in a specific festival.

My other piece of advice would be, "Don't go there in a third- or forth-tier festival, or the sidebar of the sidebar of the sidebar, where they're projecting films on a sheet, just to be in Park City." You may in fact be the undiscovered gem, but in those events, you have little or no chance of actually getting discovered by people that ultimately matter to the future success of your film.

Tiffany Shlain
Director (San Francisco)

Tiffany Shlain is an award-winning filmmaker, the founder and creative director of The Webby Awards, and the on-air Internet expert for *Good Morning, America*. Honoured as one of *Newsweek's* "Women Shaping the 21st Century," she has pioneered many unique productions in both film and theatre. Her recent projects include the film *Less Is Moore*, about the life of Gordon Moore, narrated by Harrison Ford; a theatre production starring Alan Cumming at the San Francisco Opera House; and the experimental film *Natural Connection*, about the evolution of our relationship to technology.

Tiffany received her B.A. in film theory from the University of California Berkeley in 1992, where she earned the highest award in art for her filmmaking and was selected as valedictorian speaker. She studied filmmaking at NYU in 1991. She has received awards for her filmmaking, creative direction, and leadership in the technology and entertainment industries. Tiffany is currently working on a recent film commission to explore the decline in voting by young Americans.

BC: Your documentary *Life, Liberty & The Pursuit of Happiness* was at the 2003 festival. Was this your first trip to Sundance?

TS: Yes, it was my first attempt, and I was so thrilled to get in.

BC: What were your first impressions of the festival?

TS: The staff at the festival were just wonderful, and there was a kind of very exciting energy to it all. It was also brilliant to be able to meet all the other filmmakers. I think I described it as like getting the "golden ticket" in *Willy Wonka and the Chocolate Factory*.

BC: How did you find Park City itself — did it meet your expectations?

TS: When we finally got to the town, I didn't really know what to expect. Everything was quite far apart, but I did think the town was really quaint. I guess I didn't really have an expectation...

BC: What sort of preparation was involved in going to Sundance with a film in the official program?

TS: I hired an experienced publicist to help us with the film, just to deal with that aspect of it. She was doing other films there as well, so ours was just a little gig for her. Having a publicist was especially helpful because she was really in the know about what was going on and was able to give us some inside skinny that we wouldn't have otherwise had. She also organised a lot of interviews for me when I was there. So hiring a publicist for the film and going to several Sundance orientations were kind of all the prep I did. I guess I also spent a lot of time on the Sundance Web site trying to figure out what other films to see. I was really excited about the possibility of seeing other films at Sundance, but I think that part was a little frustrating, though... the Web site, getting tickets to the festival, and so on. I think they got that feedback from a lot of people, and they might have revamped that now.

BC: How was it that Life, Liberty & The Pursuit of Happiness came to be selected for the festival?

TS: I just entered it. I didn't know anyone at the festival; I didn't have any contacts. I was a little nervous at first — I'd heard that it was difficult to get in without knowing someone, but I just entered it, and that's how it got in.

BC: That's the way it should be, I guess.

TS: Yes, exactly. It was even more validating on that level because everyone else had said, "I know so and so and can have them put in a good word for you." But I was just like, "I'm simply going to throw this up to the wind and see what happens."

BC: Was there any specific preparation you had to do for the

Park City screenings themselves, or did the festival sort that out for you?

TS: The festival looked after all of that stuff for me. My film was actually on Beta SP, so I had to get it transferred to a different format because the festival didn't screen Beta SP. But other than that, it was all pretty straightforward. I felt very well taken care of, and there were a lot of people who were very supportive of my film. That was great because my film is a political film in a time when our country is heading down the wrong path. Actually, that was the other prep... because the film is about reproductive rights, we did work with the Planned Parenthood organisation in Utah ahead of the festival. We made an effort to get in touch with people in the local community via Planned Parenthood Utah who did an event for the film. It was nice to have this kind of community outreach.

BC: How was the audience response to the film in Park City?

TS: It was great — every screening was packed. The film is a short, and it was programmed really well with a feature film that truly complemented it. I was glad the film was shown in front of a feature as opposed to being in a shorts program because I think it was just a better experience for all concerned. I guess there are pros and cons for both ways, but I was really happy with the film they programmed my film with.

BC: Yeah, I think that if you're in amongst a collection of other shorts, the other films around you can influence the audience's reaction to your film.

TS: Yeah. So it was just nice to be with a feature.

BC: The subject matter of your film is potentially controversial to some people. Did you get any interesting questions in the post-screening Q&A?

TS: The Q&A sessions were great. We had some real film enthusiasts in the audience — a really intelligent audience. One of the screenings turned into a bit of a political rally. We had Al Gore there, and the energy in the room was just palpable.

BC: Were the questions mainly around filmmaking, or did the film's subject matter provoke more of a debate?

TS: I would say the balance between questions on filmmaking and questions on the subject matter was pretty even.

BC: Do you have any memorable anecdotes from your experience at the festival?

TS: There were a couple of highlights... with the help of Planned Parenthood, we created these kind of Sundance Survival Kits, all about safe sex. They had a condom, lube, and a whole bunch of other stuff. It was pretty funny handing those out in the Mormon capital. I also think that inviting Al Gore to the screening and having him come was a big highlight, and the Sundance programmer Roberta Monroe did a wonderful intro for that screening. It was definitely a peak experience in my life — my parents flew in, all my friends were there, the crew were there, the cast was there, Al Gore was there... it was great.

Another wonderful thing... I said before how I felt like I'd got the "golden ticket" to the chocolate factory — that was the closest analogy I could come up with to describe the Sundance experience. Later on, I found out that Mel Stuart, the director of Willy Wonka and the Chocolate Factory, had actually been to one of the screenings and really loved the film, so that was icing on the cake.

Something else that was really great was the orientation session they had for Sundance selectees in L.A. a month before the festival. Besides getting to meet the other filmmakers, which was brilliant, the head of the festival [Geoff Gilmore] just gave this incredibly inspirational talk. He said that each programmer had to really believe in each film they selected and fight for it to be included. So that was an incredible moment to learn how passionate the Sundance programmers were for our films. That was definitely a highlight.

BC: Did you find any favourite places to eat when you were in Park City?

TS: Chez Betty was a great place to eat. It was on the ground floor of the condo complex we were staying in, so the convenience was great. All the food in Park City was pretty incredible, though.

BC: What about places to network and socialise? Did you find yourself spending time in one place more than others?

TS: I hung out a bit at the Sundance House, and the House of Docs [now Filmmaker Lodge] was pretty cool. But other than that, nowhere particular. I was around, just trying to make it to the various screenings and different places.

BC: From your experiences at the festival this year [2003], would you have any advice for future Sundance virgins?

TS: Before the festival, I went to an orientation in San Francisco which was organised by our Film Arts Foundation, and that was really helpful. So I would highly recommend either going to an orientation or trying to find someone who has been to Sundance before to give you advice. I would say it's really key as it helps you get a lay of the land, and that just makes it so much easier when you're there.

Jeremy Wooding
Director (UK)

Following his graduation from Manchester University with a degree in German and drama, British directory Jeremy Wooding completed a M.A. in film and television at Middlesex University. He has worked extensively in Germany: teaching English and drama, running an English-language theatre company, and as an assistant director on TV soaps. Following further work as an assistant director in the U.K., Jeremy began directing pop promos and commercials. His most recent work for television was directing the Channel 4 (U.K.) series *Derren Brown: Mind Control*, which won the Silver Rose at the Montreux International Television Awards in 2003. He also directed a new comedy/drama series for Channel 4 called *Peep Show*, which aired in autumn 2003.

Bollywood Queen is his first feature, which he co-wrote with Neil Spencer.

As a filmmaker, Jeremy describes himself as primarily coming out of the vibrant independent short-film scene in London, where filmmakers often finance and produce their own films. This independent spirit led to the *London Love Trilogy*, consisting of *Soul Patrol*, a comedy/horror romance starring Sadie Frost, Davinia Taylor, and Clint Dyer; *Sari & Trainers*; and Paris, Brixton, shown both theatrically and on Channel 4's shorts showcase, *The Shooting Gallery*. *Sari & Trainers* was the inspiration behind *Bollywood Queen* and won the Audience Award at the Halloween Society Bollywood U.K. Festival.

BC: Your film *Bollywood Queen* was selected for the World Cinema program at the 2003 festival. Was that your first trip to Sundance?

JW: It was the first trip to Sundance and my third time to America.

BC: How did you find the festival and the city itself?

JW: Well, for a start, it's a long way to go from Britain. When I arrived in Chicago, it already felt like enough, but there was still another stretch after that. To a certain extent, it did feel like going to the other side of the world, but that's part of the charm as well. It's so on its own, both as a festival and a place, and it was very interesting once I arrived there because I didn't really know what to expect. People said, "Sundance? Oh, that's Park City. It's in a ski resort," and I'm like, "Well, what's Park City? Is it a bunch of chalets? Is it a village? How big is it?" Eventually, I talked to a few people who had been there before, and someone described it to me as "basically one long street with a whole bunch of bars on it."

My first experience on arriving in Park City was that things were a bit disorganised. I got in quite late, and when I went to the desk I was supposed to report to, there wasn't anyone there. I ended up having to wait around for quite a bit of time before one of the organisers just happened to walk past. Everyone is fairly laid back there, which is fine, but it did feel a little haphazard for a major film festival. In the end, everything was fine, and once you were in, these eccentricities and this quirkiness sort of made sense. It did take me about a day or two to figure out the whole setup, but I ended up really liking the relaxed nature of the festival.

The bus system was great, too — I really liked the fact you could jump on and off and that you could meet the audience on the bus. And since you have these identity tags, people can see which film you are involved with, so they tell you what they thought of your film. This was also great for meeting other filmmakers because you could start chatting to them about their films as well.

BC: I definitely think one of the best things about the festival is the bus system because it has a social aspect to it as well as the practical aspect.

JW: Yeah, it does. I met the *Raising Victor Vargas* crowd — some cast and crew — on the bus one day. That was really nice because they were a wonderfully chilled-out bunch of people. But I think the best thing was standing on the bus and just

having someone from the audience say, "I saw your movie yesterday," or "I'm going to see your movie," or "I heard good things about your movie." This sort of instant feedback from the audience is great. And I think American audiences are a bit more open about telling you what they think than perhaps European audiences are.

BC: Knowing that you were heading to Park City with a film in the official program, what sort of preparation did you do ahead of the festival?

JW: Most of the preparation was looked after by my sales agents. They organised a party for the film and all the stuff for the screenings. What ended up being the most difficult for me was the fact that I suddenly had a lot of cast and crew wanting to go over, and of course the festival was only paying for me to go. They had loads of questions for me like, "How do we get there? Where do we stay?" and so on. I wasn't able to tell them very much, so it all got a bit frantic at one point. In the end, I just had to say to them, "Talk to the co-ordinators, and they'll tell you what it's all about."

BC: How did a typical day pan out for you while you were in Park City?

JW: Well, at the time, I was in the middle of a television production in Britain, so I was partly going to the festival as a holiday. Most of our screenings weren't until lunchtime or the afternoon, so I was able to get up late most days. The press stuff also wasn't arranged until the afternoon. I had a publicist working with me who was looking after my schedule — a lady from Denis Davidson Associates called Mia Farrell, who was very good. So a typical day involved not getting up particularly early, having a nice leisurely breakfast, jumping on the bus, and heading into town to meet cast and crew.

I have to say I never did manage to see any movies in Park City. I did try to go to a couple of screenings, but something would always come up at the last minute, either an interview or a meeting with some buyers, that sort of thing. So I didn't end up seeing any films apart from my own four times. It was a shame really as there were some great movies to see there. I think some people thought it was odd that I hadn't managed to go and see any of these movies, but I wasn't really there to see as many movies as possible — I was there to represent my film and have a bit of a holiday.

BC: I think a lot of major festivals are like that for people who are attending with a business agenda — and I would include having a film in the official program as a business agenda...

JW: Yeah. I was there working. So when I wasn't working, I didn't want to work, if you know what I mean?

BC: How was it that *Bollywood Queen* came about being selected for the festival?

JW: One of the festival programmers had seen it at Cannes in May 2002. They had spoken to our sales agent and expressed an interest in my movie. At that point, we were in the middle of doing some reshoots, so we promised to send them a copy once

we were back in the edit suite. We stayed in contact, and in November 2002, we sent them a rough copy straight off the Avid suite. I was really worried about it because the sound wasn't mixed, the grading was terrible, and so on. A week or two later, I got a message on my answer phone at home from the programmer saying, "I've got some good news for you... you've been selected for the World Cinema section of Sundance." I was just on Cloud Nine for the rest of the day because I'd never dreamed of going to Sundance before. I never thought of even entering it because for me Sundance was an American independent festival, and I didn't think they were interested in Brit movies. It was an amazing feeling to receive the call because one of the best things about being in Sundance is that it does bring great recognition for your work. Because it's so hard to make independent films, having someone say, "Hey, you've done all right, and we recognise that," is worth a hell of a lot — it gives you the strength to carry on.

BC: So what was involved in preparing to screen the film in the festival?

JW: Well, that was all taken care of by the sales agent... getting the film print there, getting the posters sorted out, and all that stuff. My sales agent is in Australia, Arclight Films, and I know it was also a big year for them at Sundance with two movies in the official program. They organised a great, but fairly low-key, party for us and also produced a freebie sampler CD for the movie. *Bollywood Queen* is of course a musical, so we had around 300 CDs produced in London, and I took them with me.

We also had some t-shirts left over from Cannes, which I also took, so my bags were really weighed down with marketing stuff.

BC: How was Bollywood Queen received at its screenings?

JW: I was kind of excited and petrified at the same time because it was an American audience, and Bollywood Queen is a particularly offbeat kind of British movie. It has a British/Asian aspect to it, and I just didn't know how the American audience would react to that. The first screening was in the Egyptian Theater, which is an old theatre and very cavernous. I have to say the sound system in that theatre wasn't brilliant, and a few people came up to me after the screening and said, "We couldn't understand the English. You'll have to do what they did with The Full Monty and dub it for an American release." Clearly I was a bit worried about that, but then at the other four screenings, I never heard that comment again. The reason was simply because the other theatres had better sound systems. The problem in the Egyptian was simply that the audience couldn't hear it properly — the system was too basey and too rumbley — but the other screenings were fine. So it was a big relief that they could understand the English and Scottish accents — the Americans went for it big time.

The screening we had in Salt Lake City was particularly amazing because you get a lot of students there, and that created a completely different vibe to Park City. I did a brief intro, and then the audience just went for it. They laughed... interestingly enough, they laughed at all of the stuff which had references to America or Americana in it. That was a real eye-opener for me. I found myself thinking, "This is what an American audience looks for — some way of understanding another culture through their own culture." Everyone also stayed for the Q&A sessions after the screenings, and those were brilliant. People were very forthcoming and very receptive to it, and that was great for me as a filmmaker planning an American release.

BC: You touched a bit on the Q&A sessions there. Did you get any memorable questions, either because you felt they were well thought out or even because you weren't prepared for them?

JW: There were a couple of punchy questions... basically the same stuff I'd had before with the short film, things like, "What's a white guy doing a movie like this for?" and "Why aren't there more Asian names in the cast and crew?" There was one particular guy who said this at the Egyptian Theater screening — a white guy. I ended up having to say, "Look, I don't make Indian movies. I'm not an Indian director, and this crew doesn't come from India. And who are you to say whether someone is black, white, pink, or purple? In fact, my continuity person is German, my DOP is a New Zealander... the movie is a multicultural movie, and that's also reflected in the cast and crew." The whole theatre burst into applause at that. Sometimes I think you just need to set people straight and say, "This is what it's like in London — this is my culture."

So the Q&A sessions were mostly very interesting, although the same kind of questions tended to keep coming up. Most people were very interested in where it all came from and what the whole Bollywood culture was about. I also had four of the actors onstage with me during the Q&A sessions, which was great because they could field some questions, and that helped keep it very lively.

BC: Did the film actually get picked up at Sundance?

JW: No, it wasn't. A lot of people came to see it, people like Miramax, Fox Searchlight... I think executives from most of the companies who were in Park City. After a screening, I'd see my sales agent in a huddle with these guys, but nobody picked it up. There were deals on the table, but I don't think the deals were good enough. We ended up making the decision to wait for the U.K. release, see how it went there, and then build on that for a better price in the U.S.

But the whole process was really interesting for me because I got to meet a lot of distributors face to face. I have to say that they weren't really that interested in meeting me; they were just interested in talking business with the sales executives. It was a bit like, "Ooo... a filmmaker. Bloody hell. Don't talk to him... we might need to tell him what we think of the movie!" It was a bit odd because by that point, I'd gotten used to the openness of Sundance and just chatting to people whenever. But it was nice to be able to meet a couple of studio execs from L.A. and a couple of agents from ICM and William Morris, who had approached me through our publicist. I had nice chats with them as well, and they were very interesting. I did take it all with a pinch of salt because I knew they were just doing their thing, but it was nice to be hunted down and buttonholed a bit.

BC: Do you have a memorable anecdote from your experience at the festival that you like to recount?

JW: Well, a lot of it has to do with seeing famous people because they're just walking around town like they live there. One day, I was getting a coffee in Starbucks, and there was Renée Zellweger standing in front of me, or another day sitting in a restaurant next to Steve Buscemi. I went to the *Spun* party — the film *Spun* — which was really cool. They were showing this behind-the-scenes footage of Mena Suvari and Brittany Murphy pole-dancing virtually naked. I remember thinking, "Wow, if the movie's all like this, it's going to be great," but everyone said, "No, it's not like this. This is better than the movie."

I also really liked the food and drink in Park City... but it was funny about this whole "Utah licensing laws" thing you're warned so much about. You know, "It's impossible to get a drink," and all that. Well, it's easier to get a drink in Utah than it is in London! Everything is open until late, and there are loads of choices. I did have one odd licensing-law experience, though — I was having a meal with a few of the cast and crew at a restaurant one night, quite a swanky restaurant on Main Street. I ordered two bottles of wine for the table and also asked the waiter if we could have a bottle of champagne to start with. The manager sort of sidled up to me and said, "I'm very sorry, sir, but we can only have one bottle of wine on the table at a time." I went, "Why?" And he said, "Because it's state law." That was very odd.

The other thing that was really funny was a trip home one night in one of these huge SUV taxies. We got into one which happened to be a karaoke taxi — the driver puts on this disc, and there are little DVD screens in the back, and you pass the mic around. We just had a wicked time. And because my movie's a musical, I was there with four brilliant singers. The party was in the taxi — not where we ended up!

BC: Did you find any places that were good for networking or socialising?

JW: Pretty much anywhere that was associated with the festival. The Filmmaker Lodge was really great — I liked having coffee in there and chatting to people. It had a really nice feel to it. The bar at the Yarrow Hotel was also great at night. You could meet people there who weren't necessarily filmmakers — just festivalgoers or other people. I also found that Starbucks was brilliant. Even though there was nowhere to sit, it was basically just meeting people in line. I also quite liked the fact that there were bars in town which weren't anything to do with the festival, but still put on a great night for festivalgoers.

BC: Would you have any advice for future Sundance virgins?

JW: Well, I think my main advice would be to get your festival tickets early. Everyone logs onto the Web site as soon as they're available, and the tickets seem to go very quickly. Also get your condo, flat, or whatever sorted out early; and it doesn't have to be expensive — that's what I found out. A lot of the Web sites for accommodation show what are pretty much premium rates, but there are plenty of places that aren't that expensive. If you're staying slightly outside of Park City but still on the bus route, it's really quick to get around, and the buses run until one in the morning, which is brilliant. So I think if you're worried about cost, it's not a big problem if you can't find anything in the centre of Park City, although I wouldn't recommend staying in Salt Lake City. I think that's a mistake because you do really feel out of it. But just outside Park City is fine. And, yeah, take some warm clothing.

the
appendices

---

appendix i

further info

Sundance — A Festival Virgin's Guide contains a large amount of information, but that doesn't mean you should stop here. There are many excellent resources that will also help with your visit to Park City and provide useful or interesting information about the festival.

On the Web

SFVG Online
The official Web site for *Sundance — A Festival Virgin's Guide* contains a series of useful tools and a wealth of additional information. Visit the site to get the latest festival news, meet other Sundance contacts, submit your own tips, and access a range of features to help you get the most out of your visit:

• Festival Information — updates and the latest buzz on the next festival

• Accommodation Exchange — free message boards to find or offer Park City accommodation

• Restaurant Guide — the lowdown on the best places to eat in Park City for all budgets

• Travel Desk — good deals on flights to the festival

• Message Boards — a place to share information and meet new Sundance contacts

Sundance — A Festival Virgin's Guide Online is available at www.sundanceguide.net

Official Festival Site

Sundance Institute
The Sundance Web site provides information about the institute and the festival. An official festival Web site is also launched via the institute site in October each year for the next festival. *www.sundance.org*

Guides and Other Useful Sites

Park City Chamber of Commerce and Visitors Bureau
The official site for the Park City tourist office provides a range of information about visiting the town, including accommodation, nightlife, arts and culture, and of course winter sports. *www.parkcityinfo.com*

Park City Official Site
The official site of the town of Park City provides access to in-depth information for visitors, residents, and businesses. *www.parkcity.org*

Filmfestivals.com
Covering many film festivals, including Sundance, filmfestivals.com contains a huge amount of information and has dedicated coverage leading up to and during the event. *www.filmfestivals.com*

News and Media Coverage

indieWIRE
In addition to being the only media outlet that publishes a Sundance-dedicated daily, indieWIRE provides the latest news, reviews, interviews, and gossip on its Web site. *www.indiewire.com*

Variety and The Hollywood Reporter
The two leading industry trade magazines provide extensive

coverage of the festival through their Web sites, although to access the content in detail, you normally need to be a subscriber. *www.variety.com /www.hollywoodreporter.com*

Screen Daily
This publication offers coverage of the festival from an international perspective. The online offering from Screen International is now a subscription service; however, the rates are reasonable and the reporting extensive. *www.screendaily.com*

Recommended Reading

The following books provide a great way to explore the fascinating topic of the Sundance Film Festival further, along with the history and culture surrounding it. All of these books and more are available from the SFVG Shop at www.sundanceguide.net

Marketing and Selling Your Film Around the World: A Guide for Independent Filmmakers
By John Durie, Annika Pham, and Neil Watson

The Ultimate Film Festival Survival Guide
By Chris Gore

Sundancing: Hanging Out and Listening In at America's Most Important Film Festival
By John Anderson and David Morgan

Sundance to Sarajevo: Film Festivals and the World They Made
By Kenneth Turan

Party in a Box: The Story of the Sundance Film Festival
By Lory Smith

International Film Festival Guide
Edited by Shael Stolberg

Lonely Planet USA
Edited by James Lyon

Let's Go USA
By Let's Go Inc.

appendix ii
sundance black book

Building up a little black book of Park City contacts can take a large amount of time. Thankfully, SFVG has made a start for you...

Official Contacts

Sundance Institute
P.O. Box 3630
Salt Lake City, UT 84110-3630
U.S.A.
Tel. 801-328-3456
Fax. 801-575-5175
www.sundance.org

General Enquiries:
institute@sundance.org

Press Office:
press@sundance.org

Volunteer Office:
volunteers@sundance.org

Festival Submissions:
programming@sundance.org

Festival Customer Service:
festivalinfo@sundance.org

Box Office
festivalregistration@sundance.org

Festival Box Office, Park City
Gateway Center
136 Heber Avenue

Festival Box Office, Salt Lake City
Trolley Square
700 East 500 South, second level

Alternative Festival Contacts

Slamdance
5634 Melrose Ave.
Los Angeles, CA 90038
U.S.A.
Tel. 323-466-1786
Fax. 323-466-1784
www.slamdance.com

Nodance Film and Multimedia Festival
703 Pier Avenue #675
Hermosa Beach, CA 90254
U.S.A.
Tel. 310-964-0700
www.nodance.com

Slamdunk Film Festival
202 Main Street, Suite 14
Venice, CA 90291
U.S.A.
Tel. 310-399-3358
Fax. 310-399-8909
www.slamdunk.cc

X-Dance
www.x-dance.com

Tromadance
www.tromadance.com

Cafés and Restaurants

350 Main Brasserie
350 Main Street
Tel. 435-649-3140

Blind Dog Grill
1781 Sidewinder Drive
Tel. 435-655-0800
Burgies
570 Main Street
Tel. 435-649-0011

Chenéz
710 Lower Main Street
Tel. 435-940-1909

Chimayo
368 Main Street
Tel. 435-649-6222

Cisero's
306 Main Street
Tel. 435-649-5044

The Claimjumper
573 Main Street
Tel. 435-649-8051

The Corner Café
1800 Park Avenue
Tel. 435-649-7000

Davanza's Pizzeria
690 Park Avenue
Tel. 435-649-2222

The Eating Establishment
317 Main Street
Tel. 435-649-8284

El Chubasco
1890 Bonanza Drive
Tel. 435-645-9114

Goldener Hirsch Inn
7570 Royal Street East
Tel. 435-649-7770

Grappa
151 Main Street
Tel. 435-645-0636

La Casita
710 Lower Main Street
Tel. 435-645-9585
Lakota
751 Lower Main Street
Tel. 435-658-3400

Main Street Deli
525 Main Street
Tel. 435-649-1110

Main Street Pizza & Noodle
530 Main Street
Tel. 435-645-8878

Mariposa
7620 Royal Street East
Tel. 435-645-6715

Morning Ray Café and Bakery
275 Main Street
Tel. 435-649-5686

Mountain Chicken
1890 Bonanza Drive
Tel. 435-645-8483

Off Main Café and Bakery
1782 Prospector Ave
Tel. 435-649-6478

Red Banjo Pizza
322 Main Street
Tel. 435-649-9901

Sai-Sommet
7720 Royal Street East
Tel. 435-645-9909

Wasatch Brew Pub
250 Main Street
Tel. 435-649-9500

Windy Ridge Café
1250 Iron Horse Drive
Tel. 435-647-0880

Wok on Main
438 Main Street
Tel. 435-649-0957
Zoom
660 Lower Main Street
Tel. 435-649-9108

Park City Contacts

Emergency
Tel. 911
(Police/Fire/Medical)

Avalanche Report
Tel. 801-364-1581

Department of Motor Vehicles
Tel. 800-368-8824

Highway Conditions
Tel. 801-964-6000

Highway Patrol
Tel. 435-655-3445

Park City Library
Tel. 435-615-5600

Park City Police Department
Tel. 435-615-5500

Park City Visitor Information Center
Tel. 435-658-4541

Albertsons (supermarket)
Tel. 435-649-6134

Albertsons Pharmacy
Tel. 435-649-6264

Dan's Pharmacy
Tel. 435-645-7916

Rite Aid Pharmacy
Tel. 435-649-9621

Poison Control
Tel. 800-456-7707

Sheriff's Department
Tel. 435-615-3500

Snow Creek Emergency & Medical Center
Tel. 435-655-0055

Park City Family Health (Doctor)
Tel. 435-649-7640

University of Utah Summit Clinic (Doctor)
Tel. 435-647-5740

Taxi Services

ACE Cab Company
Tel. 435-649-8294

Citiride Taxi Service
Tel. 435-658-2220

Music Taxi
Tel. 435-649-6496

Park City Cabs
Tel. 435-658-2227

Powder for the People
Tel. 435-649-6648

State Liquor Stores

Prospector Square
The largest liquor store in Park City, with one of the most extensive wine selections in Utah. Open 10am–10pm, Monday to Saturday. Closed Sundays. 1901 Sidewinder Drive. Tel. 435-649-7254

Historic District
A smaller store, situated about halfway up Main Street. Open 11am–10pm, Monday to Saturday. Closed Sundays. 524 Main Street. Tel. 435-649-3293

Photocopy and Fax

Copy Depot
875 Iron Horse Drive
Tel. 435-649-2679
www.pccopydepot.com

Printing PC
1733 Sidewinder Drive
Tel. 435-649-7400

Internet Café

Alpine Internet Coffeehouse
738 Lower Main Street
Tel. 435 649 0051
www.alpineinternet.net

Major International Film Markets

American Film Market (AFM)
10850 Wilshire Boulevard, 9th Floor
Los Angeles, CA 90024-4311
U.S.A.
Tel. 310-446-1000
Fax. 310-446-1600
www.americanfilmmarket.com

Marché du Film (Cannes)
3, rue Amélie
75007 Paris
France
Tel. +33 1 53 59 61 30
Fax. +33 1 53 59 61 50
www.cannesmarket.com

MIFED (Milan)
FMI — Fiera Milano International
Palazzina FMI
Largo Domodossola 1
20145 Milan
Italy
Tel. +39 2 485 501
Fax. +39 2 4855 0420
www.mifed.com

Trade Magazines

The Hollywood Reporter
5055 Wilshire Boulevard
Los Angeles, CA 90036-4396
U.S.A.
Tel. 323-525-2000
Fax. 323-525-2377
www.hollywoodreporter.com

indieWIRE
601 West 26th Street, Suite 1150
New York, NY 10001
U.S.A.
Tel. 212-320-3710
Fax. 212-320-3719
www.indiewire.com

Moving Pictures International
2 Chitty Street
London W1T 4AP
United Kingdom
Tel. +44 20 7813 9506
Fax. + 44 20 7813 9500
www.movingpicturesonline.com

Screen International
33-39 Bowling Green Lane
London, EC1R 0DA
United Kingdom
Tel. +44 20 7505 8080
www.screendaily.com

Variety
5700 Wilshire Boulevard, Suite 120
Los Angeles, CA 90036
U.S.A.
Tel. 323-857-6600
Fax. 323-857-0494
www.variety.com

appendix iii
alternative festivals

The explosion in popularity of the Sundance Film Festival in the 1990s brought with it an interesting dilemma: the more popular the festival became, the higher the number of film submissions went, and consequently, the percentage of those selected grew smaller and smaller. Much like what happened at other high-profile festivals, it was only a matter of time before alternative events sprang up to cater to this overflow.

Today, the Sundance Film Festival plays somewhat reluctant host to possibly the largest number of "coattail events" of any major international film festival. These range from established regular events like Slamdance, Nodance, and Slamdunk to more specialised affairs like X-Dance or Tromadance. Many of these alternative festivals have blossomed into year-round events and pop up in various forms at other major international film festivals, as well as run competitions, educational programs, and even small distribution operations.

In addition to these events, most years at Sundance see a slate of more amorphous offerings that usually stick around for one or two festivals before disappearing into the annals of Park City history. Some of the more memorable events have included Roadance (maximum mobility using rear projection to screen films on the back of a truck), Slumdance (enjoy your cinema in a mock slum), Sleazedance (trying hard to replicate the success of Cannes' Hot d'Or), and even Onedance (the brainchild of a disgruntled filmmaker whose work missed being a Sundance selection, so he decided to stage his own festival to show his film).

Slamdance
Slamdance has come a long way from its beginnings as an event famously described as "born out of rejection." Started in 1995 by a group of upstart young filmmakers, Slamdance has built a reputation for premiering independent films from first-time directors who work with limited budgets. The Slamdance Film Festival runs in Park City from mid- to late-January each year alongside Sundance and includes a feature-film competition (for both dramatic and documentary works), a series of special screenings, and a video shorts and documentary showcase known as The Lounge Screenings. Aside from a two-year stint at the Silver Mine, Slamdance has always taken place at the Treasure Mountain Inn at the top of Main Street. For more information on Slamdance, visit the official Web site at www.slamdance.com.

Nodance
The self-proclaimed "third" film festival in Park City takes a subtle dig at the standard "dance" nomenclature of the other alternative events by simultaneously using it and suggesting it isn't there. Launched in 1998, Nodance, much like Slamdance, was also born out of rejection (although ironically by both Sundance AND Slamdance). Nodance describes itself as a festival which celebrates alternative digital film culture, with an emphasis on first-time filmmakers

and digital filmmaking, and includes competitions for features and shorts and a series of special screenings. Nodance is based upstairs in the Park City Mall on Main Street (opposite the Egyptian Theater) and runs for one week in January alongside Sundance. For more information on Nodance and submission details, visit the official festival Web site at www. nodance.com.

Slamdunk

Taking its first bow in 1998, Slamdunk is focused on showcasing short and feature films from new and established talent in the independent sector and has become a travelling event with an (unofficial) presence at many of the top international film festivals, including Cannes, Sundance, and Toronto. The Park City event hosts around 12 feature films and a couple of dozen shorts each year, along with a series of panel events. Slamdunk has moved around among a variety of venues in Park City during its history — its most recent home was the basement of Harry O's on Main Street for the 2003 festival. Check the official Web site at www.slamdunk.cc for more information.

Others

In addition to more established alternative events, a slate of newcomers have started to become regular fixtures on the scene. These include X-Dance, aimed at "elevating action sports films, taking them to the next level of Hollywood recognition and mass market appeal"; and Tromadance — a four-day showcase of no-budget shorts and short features from schlock-horror guru Lloyd Kaufman's Troma Entertainment.

The venues for these events are subject to change, so it's always a good idea to check their Web sites ahead of the next festival (see Appendix II).

appendix iv
mobile phones 101

In recent years, the mobile phone (aka cell phone) has become an essential piece of kit for most professionals, filmmakers among them. If you're heading to Sundance with any business objectives in mind, being contactable at all times is paramount. Fortunately, the pioneers of mobile phone technology had the foresight to realise that people might want to take their phones with them when they travel to new cities, and even new countries.

Through a myriad of deals between national and international telecommunications companies, most mobile phones can now be used in major population centres all over the world. The phone-industry jargon for this ability is "roaming." In an ideal world, any phone would be able to roam in any city or country without a problem; however, whilst the vision driving the telecommunications industry was able to deliver the potential to use any phone anywhere, the economics has stopped it somewhat short of ubiquity. So the most important question is, will your phone work in Park City?

For festivalgoers who are heading to Sundance from another part of North America, there is little to worry about, assuming you have a digital handset, and there are no operator or other call bars in place. Calls may be a little more expensive than they are at home since many phone companies surcharge you for the privilege of roaming, but other than that, everything should be fine. For international visitors, on the other hand, several complications add to the mix.

To understand some of these issues, we need to take a moment to examine the most common technologies which drive digital mobile phones today. Across the world, two (incompatible) standards dominate the market for digital phone services. These are known as CDMA (Code Division Multiple Access) and GSM (Global System for Mobile Communications). Whilst approximately 70 percent of the world's mobile phones use the GSM standard, CDMA is by far the leading system in North America. Historically, this part of the world was slower to adopt digital mobile phone technology, so market conditions as well as geography pushed the U.S. into adopting CDMA. The coverage and user base of GSM networks in North America is growing, but it still has a long way to go before it overtakes CDMA.

Most phones in Europe, Australasia, and the Far East use the GSM standard; however, an additional complication stands in the way of all GSM phones working in North America. For reasons which I'm sure make sense to the techies who developed them, there are now three variations of the GSM standard in use across the world. These are GSM 900 (named because it uses the 900 MHz radio frequency); GSM 1800 (sometimes called PCN); and GSM 1900 (1900 MHz). Of the three standards, only GSM 1900 is used in North America, so for your GSM phone to work in Park City, it needs to support the GSM 1900 standard. Non-U.S. phones that do this are generally called "tri-band", since they support 900, 1800, and 1900 MHz communications. (Note that most "dual-band" GSM phones are usually 900/1800, and therefore not suitable for use in the U.S.).

To find out which standards your phone supports, either refer to the phone's operating manual or contact your service provider. Most mobile operators provide detailed information about international roaming on their Web sites, normally including coverage and cost details.

Park City Coverage
The main providers of mobile phone coverage in the Park City area are:

T-Mobile (GSM 1900)
(aka VoiceStream)
www.t-mobile.com

Cingular (GSM 1900)
www.cingular.com

SprintPCS (CDMA)
www.sprintpcs.com

Making/Receiving Calls When Roaming (U.S. Phones)
If you're heading to Park City from another part of the U.S., there are no special requirements if you have a CDMA or GSM 1900 phone. Calls may be a little more expensive because your phone company charges its roaming fees, but other than that, you should be able to make and receive calls normally.

Making Calls When Roaming (International Phones)
When making calls, even if they are local, you must dial the number as if it was international. For example, to call the local Avalanche Report, you need to dial the U.S. international access code (001), followed by the country code for the U.S.A. (1), and finally the number (801-364-1581). This is instead of the local version of the number, 801-364-1581, which you would dial from a pay or local mobile phone. Most handsets allow you to use the plus sign (+) in place of the international access code, so you can simply dial +1-801-364-1581 from your phone.

Regardless of the destination, all calls you make on your phone while roaming are charged at your phone company's international rates. This is because the host carrier you use while roaming charges your phone company for the call, and then it passes that charge, plus some of its own, on to you. Needless to say, it's probably worth keeping your calls as short as possible.

Receiving Calls (International Phones)
If you receive a call while roaming, there's also a sting in the tail. If someone in your home country calls you, or you receive a call from another person in Park City, the caller pays for the leg of the call between their location and your phone company's exchange; then you pay the remaining leg between the exchange and your location. This is of course also charged at your phone company's international rates.

To contact your phone in Park City, people in your home country simply dial the same number they would use to reach you when you're in town, and they pay standard rates for calling mobiles. However, if someone in Park City wants to call you, that person must dial your number as if it was international, using either the international access code (001) or the plus sign, your country code (i.e., 44 for the UK, 61 for Australia, etc), followed by the number, minus the leading zero. The caller pays international rates on the call between their location and your phone company's exchange; you pay the rest of the call as when someone calls you from home.

Keeping Your Bills Small(ish)

The moral of the story is that a mobile phone is an essential part of your Park City arsenal, but make sure you keep the calls (both made and received) as brief as possible. Here are several strategies that can help reduce your post-Sundance phone bill:

Set your phone to divert all calls to voice mail. This means that you only pay when you check your messages, a call that will inevitably be much cheaper than actually talking to someone. When using this strategy, make sure you have a message that makes it obvious to the caller than you will get back to them ASAP. You should also enable your phone's message-waiting indicator and carry your phone at all times. When you receive notification of a message, check it and return the call immediately (using a pay phone of course).

Use SMS services where possible. Virtually all GSM phones can send and receive SMS text messages. Although you are limited to 150 characters per message, most mobile phone operators provide this service at a fixed price per message. SMS can be an extremely cheap way of staying in touch with friends and colleagues both in Park City and at home.

Change from a prepay to contract phone. Prepay mobile phones may be cheap out of the box, but calls are often considerably more expensive than contract phones when roaming (if they can even roam at all). The other potential downside is the problem of getting your hands on top-up cards while you're away. If you do your research (and the sums), you may find that, at the end of the day, a contract phone is more flexible and cheaper to operate.

Get a local prepay phone or SIM card. Frequent travellers have learned the value of local prepay services as a way of keeping roaming bills down whilst remaining in full contact. You can either buy a local phone or simply replace the SIM card in your existing handset with one from a local prepay operator. Once you're up and running, simply let everyone know your temporary Park City number, and you're home free. Prepay phones are available in many places across town, such as convenience stores, supermarkets, and electronics shops.

Special international roaming rates. A few mobile-phone companies have started to wise up to the fact that their customers are sick of being shafted for international roaming. Contact your own mobile provider to see if any special rates exist for your phone.

Rent a phone locally. As a last resort, or if your phone just doesn't work in Park City, you can always rent a handset locally. Cell-phone rental companies in Park City are pretty thin on the ground, so you may need to locate a company in Salt Lake City instead.

More Information

The best place to start for more information on roaming (either domestic or international) is of course your phone company's Web site, but another useful site is Cellular-News. Whilst the mobile phone industry news and statistics will probably not do much more than cure your insomnia, one extremely useful feature of the site is the coverage database. This includes almost all countries and has information on phone standards and coverage maps, broken down by each operator, for the selected country and region. The direct link to the coverage area is www.cellular-news.com/coverage/.

Alternatively, visit the Web site of the U.K.'s telecommunications regulator, Oftel (www.oftel.gov.uk). Although this site is obviously targeted at British users, it provides a handy guide to keeping costs down when you're using your phone abroad, and the advice is pretty universal. Look in the Publications section under the Mobile category for a document called "Advice from Oftel on using your mobile abroad."

appendix v

accommodation booking services and hotels

Finding somewhere to stay in Park City during the festival will probably be your biggest challenge. This appendix contains an extensive list of accommodation booking services and hotels. Remember to book your accommodation as far in advance as you possibly can to get the best deal.

DESTINATION: Sundance Film Festival

In 2004, the Sundance Institute launched DESTINATION Sundance Film Festival, a one-stop travel planning service intended to simplify the process of getting yourself to Park City and having somewhere to stay when you arrive. The service is run by local travel agents and definitely worth a look.

Tel. 877-733-7829
www.destinationsff.com

Property Booking Services

ABC Reservations Central
Tel. 435-649-2223
Fax. 435-649-9948
infoue@utahescapades.com

Acclaimed Lodging
Tel. 435-649-6175
Toll-Free 800-843-8364
www.parkcitylodging.com

Accommodations Park City
Tel. 435-658-0403
Toll-Free 888-472-7524
Fax. 435-647-3055
www.accommodationsparkcity.com

All Seasons Resorts
Tel. 435-645-9626
Toll-Free 800-395-8639
www.allseasonsresorts.us

Alpine Ski Properties
Tel. 435-649-2424
Toll-Free 800-771-1505
www.alpineskiproperties.com

Altitude Resort Services
Tel. 435-615-9944
www.altitudepc.com

Anderson Apartments
Tel. 435-649-9224
Fax. 435-645-8742

Blooming Property Management
Tel. 435-649-6583
Toll-Free 800-635-4719
Fax: 435-649-6598
www.bloomingpc.com

The Canyons Central Reservations
Tel. 435-615-3360
Toll-Free 888-CANYONS
Fax. 435-615-3364
www.thecanyons.com

Central Reservations of Park City
Tel. 435-649-6606
Toll-Free 800-570-1276
Fax: 435-649-6654
www.resortquestparkcity.com/sff

China Bridge Housing
Tel. 435-649-8333

Condo Destinations
Tel. 801-466-1101
Fax. 801-466-6655
www.allpointstravelonline.com

Condominium Rentals of Park City
Tel. 435-649-2687
Toll-Free 800-221-0933
www.gotoparkcity.com

Crestview Condominiums
Tel. 435-645-3954
Toll-Free 877-838-7828
Fax: 435-649-8619
www.crestviewcondos.com

David Holland's Resort Lodging
Tel. 435-655-3315
Toll-Free 888-PARKCITY
Fax: 435-645-9132
www.davidhollands.com

Deer Valley Central Reservations
Tel. 435-649-1000
Toll-Free 800-424-DEER
Fax. 435-645-6538
www.deervalley.com

Deer Valley Lodging
Tel. 435-649-4040
Toll-Free 800-453-3833
Fax: 435-647-3318
www.deervalleylodging.com

Identity Properties
Tel. 435-649-5100
Toll-Free 800-245-6417
Fax: 435-649-5107
www.pclodge.com

Lespri Resort Property Management
Tel. 435-649-9598
Toll-Free 800-645-4762
www.resortpropertymanagement.com

A Lodging Connection
Tel. 801-905-9512
Fax. 801-905-9520
www.alodgingconnection.com

Lynx Ski Vacations
Tel. 303-355-4775 (ext. 3001)
Fax. 303-248-4441
www.lynxskivacations.com

Manassas Travel Inc
Tel. 435-940-1515
Toll-Free 800-585-2232
Fax. 435-940-1955
www.manassastravel.com

MTA Resorts
Tel. 801-531-1600
Toll-Free 800-272-UTAH
www.mtaresorts.com

Owners Resorts and Exchange
Tel. 801-278-8819
Toll-Free 800-748-4666
www.ore-inc.com
Park City Canyons Lodging
Tel. 435-645-8983
Toll-Free 800-421-5056
www.parkcitycanyonslodging.com

Park City Lodging Connection
Tel. 435-658-1535
Toll-Free 800-642-8001
Fax. 435-658-2119
www.vacationparkcity.com

Park City Mountain Resort Reservations
Tel. 435-649-8111
Toll-Free 800-222-PARK
Fax. 435-649-0532
www.parkcitymountain.com

Park City RSVP
Tel. 435-649-1592
Toll-Free 800-255-6451
Fax. 435-649-1593
www.parkcityrsvp.com
Park City Resort Lodging
Tel. 435-649-8200

Park City Travel and Lodging
Tel. 801-487-1300 or 435-645-8200
Toll-Free 800-421-9741
Fax. 801-487-2358
www.parkcitytravel.com

Park West Property Management
Tel. 435-645-8983
www.parkwestvillage.com

Premier Destinations Utah
Tel. 435-649-4800
Toll-Free 800-882-4754
Fax. 435-655-4844
www.premier-destinations.com

R&R Property Management
Tel. 435-649-6175
Toll-Free 800-348-6759
Fax: 435-649-6225
www.parkcitylodging.com

ResortQuest Park City
Tel. 435-649-6606
Toll-Free 800-570-6296
www.resortquestparkcity.com/cci

Resortside Homes
Tel. 435-731-0126
Toll-Free 800-255-6163
www.resortside.com

Resorts West
Tel. 435-655-7006
Toll-Free 800-541-9378
www.resortswest.com

Silver Cliff Village
Tel. 435-649-5500
Toll-Free 800-331-8652
www.silverkinghotel.com

Ski West, Inc
Tel. 435-655-0368
Toll-Free 866-838-3533
Fax. 435-655-9024
www.skiparkcityutah.net

Snow Flower Reservations
Tel. 435-649-6400
Toll-Free 800-852-3101
www.snowflowerparkcity.com

Snow Valley Connection
Tel. 435-645-7700
Fax. 435-645-7744
www.snowvalleyconnection.com

Snowventures
Tel. 970-453-3989
Toll-Free 800-845-7157
Fax. 970-453-3985
www.snowventures.com

Utahski.com
Tel. 480-505-5173
Toll-Free 888-349-6100
Fax. 480-505-5181
www.utahski.com

Utah Ski Reservations
Tel. 435-649-6493

Hotels and B&Bs in Park City

1904 Imperial Hotel
Tel. 435-649-1904
Toll-Free 800-669-UTAH
Fax: 435-645-7421
www.1904imperial.com

Acorn Chalets
Tel. 435-649-9313
Toll-Free 866-604-1433
Fax. 435-655-3088
www.acornchalet.com

All Seasons Condominiums
Tel. 435-649-5500
Toll-Free 800-331-8652
www.silverkinghotel.com

Alpenhof Condominiums
Tel. 801-277-4388
Fax: 801-583-1857
www.alpenhofcondos.com

Angel House Inn
Tel. 435-647-0338
Toll-Free 800-ANGEL-01
www.angelhouseinn.com

Best Western Landmark Inn
Tel. 435-649-7300
Toll-Free 800-548-8824
Fax: 435-649-1760
www.bwlandmarkinn.com

Black Bear Lodge
Tel. 435-940-0362
Toll-Free 888-727-5248
www.888parkcity.com

Blue Church Lodge and Townhouses
Tel. 435-649-8009
Toll-Free 800-626-5467

Caledonian, Town Lift and Lift Lodge
Tel. 435-649-8200
Toll-Free 800-545-7669
www.prpc.com

Carriage House Condominiums
Tel. 435-615-4600
Toll-Free 888-754-3279
www.carriagehousecondos.us

Chateau Aprés Lodge
Tel. 435-649-9372
Toll-Free 800-357-3556
Fax: 435-649-5963
www.chateauapres.com

The Chateaux at Silver Lake
Tel. 435-658-9500
Toll-Free 800-453-3833
www.chateaux-deervalley.com

Club Lespri
Tel. 435-645-9696
www.clublespri.com

Copperbottom Inn
Tel. 435-649-5111
Toll-Free 800-824-5331
www.copperbottominn.com

East West Resorts Utah
Tel. 435-658-3434
Toll-Free 800-453-5789
www.eastwestresort.com

Edelweiss Haus
Tel. 435-649-9342
Toll-Free 800-245-6417

Empire House
Tel. 435-902-9142
Toll-Free 877-275-0801
www.empirehousepc.com

The Gables
Tel. 435-658-1417
Toll-Free 800-824-5331
www.thegablespc.com

Goldener Hirsch Inn
Tel. 435-649-7770
Toll-Free 800-252-3373
Fax: 435-649-7901
www.goldenerhirschinn.com

Grand Summit Resort Hotel
Tel. 435-615-8040
Toll-Free 866-604-4170
www.thecanyons.com

Hampton Inn
Tel. 435-645-0900
Toll-Free 800-HAMPTON
Fax: 435-645-9672
www.hampton-inn.com/hi/parkcity

Holiday Inn Express Hotel
Tel. 435-658-1600
Toll-Free 800-HOLIDAY
Fax: 435-6581600
www.parkcityholidayinn.com

Hotel Park City
Tel. 435-940-5000
Toll-Free 888-999-0098
Fax: 435-940-5001
www.hotelparkcity.com

The Lodges at Deer Valley
Tel. 435-615-2600
Toll-Free 800-453-3833
www.lodge-deervalley.com

The Lodge at the Mountain Village
Tel. 435-649-0800
Toll-Free 888-PARKCITY
www.thelodgepc.com

Marriott's Mountainside Villas
Tel. 435-940-2000
Toll-Free 800-845-5279
Fax. 435-940-2010
www.vacationclub.com

Marriott Summit Watch
Tel. 435-647-4100
Toll-Free 800-223-8245
www.vacationclub.com
The Miners Club
Tel. 435-645-4400

Moose Trax at Crestview
Tel. 435-658-4486
www.crestviewcondominiums.com

Old Miners Lodge
Tel. 435-645-8068
Toll-Free 800-648-8068
Fax: 435-645-7420
www.oldminerslodge.com

Old Town Guest House
Tel. 435-649-2642
Toll-Free 800-290-6423 (ext. 3710)
Fax: 435-649-3320
www.oldtownguesthouse.com

Park City Base Camp
Tel. 435-655-7244
Toll-Free 888-980-7244
www.parkcitybasecamp.com

Park City Marriott
Tel. 435-649-2900
Toll-Free 800-234-9003
Fax: 435-649-4852
www.marriott.com/slcpc

Park Plaza Resort
Tel. 435-649-0870
Toll-Free 866-882-3866
www.parkplazaresort.com

Park Regency Hotel
Tel. 435-645-7531
Toll-Free 800-438-6493
www.extraholidays.com

Park Station Condominium Hotel
Tel. 435-649-7717
Toll-Free 888-PARKCITY
www.parkstationpc.com

Poison Creek Cottage
Toll-Free 800-779-2205
www.shire.net/poisoncreek

PowderWood Resort
Tel. 435-649-2032
Toll-Free 800-223-7829
Fax: 435-649-8619
www.powderwood.com

Prospector Square Lodge
Tel. 435-649-7100
Toll-Free 800-760-2082
www.prospectorlodging.com

Radisson Inn Park City
Tel. 435-649-5000
Toll-Free 800-649-5012
Fax. 435-649-2122
www.radisson.com/parkcityut

Shadow Ridge Resort
Tel. 435-649-4300
Toll-free 800-451-3031
Fax. 435-649-5951
www.shadowridgelodging.com

Silver King Hotel
Tel. 435-649-5500
Toll-Free 800-331-8652
Fax: 435-649-6647
www.silverkinghotel.com

Silver Queen Hotel
Tel. 435-649-5986
Toll-Free 800-447-NICE
Fax: 435-649-3572
www.silverqueenhotel.com

Star Hotel
Tel. 435-649-8333
Toll-Free 888-649-8333
www.rixey.net/starhotel

Stein Eriksen Lodge
Tel. 435-649-3700
Toll-free 800-453-1302
www.steinlodge.com
Sundial Lodge at The Canyons Resort
Tel. 435-615-8070
Toll-Free 866-604-4170
www.thecanyons.com

Trails End Lodge/Pine Inn
Tel. 435-647-3527
Toll-Free 800-453-3833
www.trailsend-deervalley.com

Treasure Mountain Inn
Tel. 435-655-4501
Toll-Free 800-344-2460
Fax: 435-655-4504
www.treasuremountaininn.com

Washington School Inn
Tel. 435-649-3800
Toll-Free 800-824-1672
Fax: 435-649-3802
www.washingtonschoolinn.com

Westgate Park City Resort and Spa
Tel. 435-940-9444
Toll-Free 888-433-3704
www.wgparkcity.com

Woodland Farmhouse Inn
Tel. 435-783-2903
Toll-Free 888-783-2903
www.woodlandfarmhouseinn.com

Woodside Inn
Tel. 435-649-3494
Toll-Free 888-241-5890
Fax: 435-649-2392
www.woodsideinn.com

The Yarrow Resort Hotel
Tel. 435-649-7000
Toll-Free 800-927-7694
Fax: 435-645-7007
www.yarrowresort.com

Hotels Near Park City

Best Western Holiday Hills (Coalville)
Tel. 435-336-4444
Toll-Free 866-922-7278
Fax. 435-336-4445
www.bwstay.com

Holiday Inn Express Heber City
Tel. 435-654-9990
Toll-Free 800-465-4329
www.hiexpress.com

appendix vi

your packing list

Travel always brings that nagging feeling of "I think I've forgotten something." If you use this checklist and bring the following items, you may be wearing the same underwear for two weeks, but at least you'll have all of the essential kit to see you successfully through Sundance.

Mobile Phone (aka cell phone)
You'll need to be in contact at all times whilst you're in Park City, and your own mobile phone is the only way to be sure. Don't rely on hotel messaging services or third parties. Bring your own phone or rent one locally.

Hangover Kit
One night you'll be partying hard into the wee hours, the next morning you'll need to be bright eyed and bushy tailed for your deal meeting. Whatever works for you, bring plenty of it.

Warm Clothes
Inevitably, you will end up spending a little time outside, particularly while you wait for a bus or line up for a screening. You'll need a warm, water-resistant jacket, a pair of gloves, and a beanie or another hat which can keep your head (and ears) warm. If you're particularly susceptible to the cold, consider clothes which you can layer.

Good Walking Boots
For most days during the festival, the ground in Park City will be covered with snow and ice. A good pair of walking boots is therefore essential to provide both grip and comfort for your feet. Walking around town in heels or trainers (aka sneakers/sandshoes/loafers) is a good way to end up on your arse.

Credit Cards
Credit cards are an essential tool for any traveller since they allow you to manage your spending more effectively and, in some cases, put off the payment pain until later. For international travellers, credit cards also bring the added bonus of more favourable exchange rates since the exchange is done by your card issuer at home rather than locally. Savvy travellers always bring at least two credit cards, just in case one doesn't work for some reason or happens to meet an untimely end.

Business Cards
You never know who you'll meet, or when, so you should carry business cards with you at all times. At minimum, they should contain your name, telephone number, and email address. Don't get bogged down with fancy job titles since they mean nothing in the film industry. At best, no one cares, and at worst, people will just think you are a prat.

Sun Protection
The cold weather in Park City can make the sun feel deceptively weak, but the reality is that you will get sunburned if you don't take the right precautions. If you're going to be spending a reasonable amount of time in the sun, you need to apply sunscreen to prevent your face turning pink. A good pair of sunnies is also a must as the glare from the snow on the ground can feel like it's melting your retinas.

Moisturiser

The air in Park City is extremely dry, and this can cause your skin to dehydrate quite quickly. The problem is particularly acute around the face, but your hands will also dry out if they spend a large part of the day inside gloves. To avoid these dry-skin problems, bring a good moisturiser and apply it daily to your face and hands.

Those coming to Park City with a film also need to pack the following materials:

Press Kit

A good press kit is essential for those who want to drum up interest in a film from either a distributor or the media. If you're working with a sales agent and/or publicist, they will have already made you go through this process; however, if you're trying it on your own, you'll have to create one yourself. A decent press kit includes a short synopsis of your film (one paragraph), a longer synopsis of your film (three to four paragraphs), bios of the principal cast and crew, one or two pages of production notes describing how your film was made, and a set of good stills (ideally in both digital and hard-copy formats).

A Disk

You should also bring a disk containing electronic versions of all your supporting materials. You may need to print more while you are in Park City, so it's always best to come armed with all the information you need.

Realistic Expectations

Perhaps the most important thing to bring with you.

about the author

Benjamin Craig started his media career at the tender age of just 18 months when he was cast as the new child of the main family in "Certain Women", a popular 1970s Australian Broadcasting Corporation (ABC) soap opera. After leaving the show aged three, Craig spent the remainder of his childhood growing up in Perth, Western Australia.

Always more comfortable behind the camera than in front of it, Craig spent much of his teens working backstage in theatre before starting a media production degree at Curtin University of Technology in 1990. Graduating in 1994 with a Bachelor of Arts (English), Craig divided his time between developing short film projects and working in the fledgling new media industry before moving to Europe in 1996.

In addition to his work in theatre, film, television, and new media, Craig is an accomplished freelance writer. He is the author of the leading film festival travel series, A Festival Virgin's Guide, with titles on the Cannes and Sundance film festivals. He has also freelanced for a variety of magazines including Vogue, GQ, and Condé Nast Traveller, and is the editor of one of the web's oldest filmmaking resources, filmmaking.net.

Benjamin Craig is currently chief executive of cross-media production company Cinemagine Media Limited and resides in London.

park city maps

This section contains two basic maps of the key areas of Park City. Free city maps are available from the tourist offices in town. Get yours as soon as you arrive.

Map 1: Main Street, Silver Lake, and Deer Valley

Map 1 shows the Main Street, Silver Lake Village, and Deer Valley areas, which lie at the southern end of town. Place names listed in bold below can be found on this map.

City Places

1. Park City Visitor Information Center
2. **Park City Historic Museum**
3. **Old Town Transit Center**
4. **Silver Mine**
5. **Snow Park Lodge**
6. Lot F Carpark
7. Lot G Carpark
8. Chateau Aprés Lodge (hotel)
9. **Park City Basecamp (hostel)**
10. Albertsons
11. 7-Eleven
12. Wells Fargo (ATM)
13. Bank One (ATM)
14. Zions Bank (ATM)
15. Park City Library

Festival Places & Cinemas

16. Festival Headquarters (HQ)
17. Park City Racquet Club
18. **Filmmaker Lodge**
19. **Sundance Digital Center**
20. **Music Café**
21. **Sundance House**
22. **Main Festival Box-Office**
23. Eccles Center
24. **Egyptian Theatre**
25. Holiday Village Cinemas
26. Prospector Theatre
27. Yarrow Hotel

Restaurants

28. **350 Main**
29. Burger King
30. Starbucks/Quiznos Sub
31. **Burgies**
32. Blind Dog
33. **La Casita**
34. **Chenéz**
35. **Chimayo**
36. **Cicero's**
37. **The Claimjumper**
38. The Corner Café
39. **Davanza's Pizzeria**
40. **The Eating Establishment**
41. El Chubasco
42. **Goldener Hirsch Inn**
43. **Grappa**
44. **Lakota**
45. **Main Street Deli**
46. **Main Street Pizza & Noodle**
47. **Mariposa**
48. Mountain Chicken
49. Off Main Café
50. Pizza Hut
51. **Red Banjo Pizza**
52. **Sai-Sommet**
53. **Wasatch Brew Pub**
54. Windy Ridge Café
55. **Wok on Main**
56. **Zoom**

Map 1: Main Street, Silver Lake, and Deer Valley

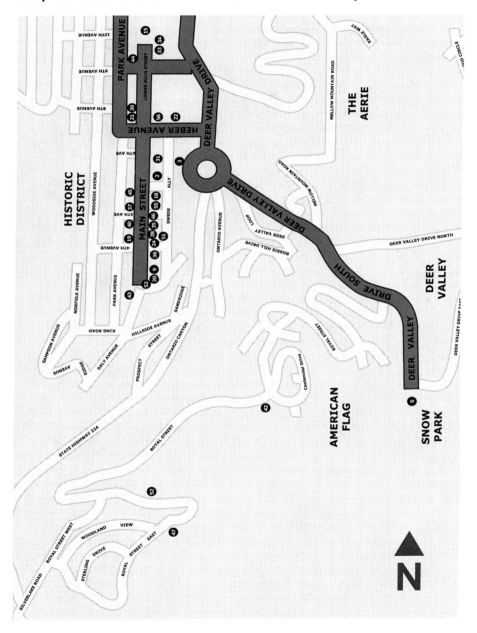

park city maps

Map 2: Prospector Square and Park Meadows

Map 2 shows the Prospector Square and Park Meadows areas, which are located at the northern end of town. Place names listed in bold below can be found on this map.

City Places

1. **Park City Visitor Information Center**
2. Park City Historic Museum
3. Old Town Transit Center
4. Silver Mine
5. Snow Park Lodge
6. **Lot F Carpark**
7. **Lot G Carpark**
8. **Chateau Aprés Lodge (hotel)**
9. Park City Basecamp (hostel)
10. **Albertsons**
11. **7-Eleven**
12. **Wells Fargo (ATM)**
13. **Bank One (ATM)**
14. **Zions Bank (ATM)**
15. **Park City Library**

Festival Places & Cinemas

16. **Festival Headquarters (HQ)**
17. **Park City Racquet Club**
18. Filmmaker Lodge
19. Sundance Digital Center
20. Music Café
21. Sundance House
22. Main Festival Box-Office
23. **Eccles Center**
24. Egyptian Theatre
25. **Holiday Village Cinemas**
26. **Prospector Theatre**
27. **Yarrow Hotel**

Restaurants

28. 350 Main
29. **Burger King**
30. **Starbucks/Quiznos Sub**
31. Burgies
32. **Blind Dog**
33. La Casita
34. Chenéz
35. Chimayo
36. Cicero's
37. The Claimjumper
38. **The Corner Café**
39. Davanza's Pizzeria
40. The Eating Establishment
41. **El Chubasco**
42. Goldener Hirsch Inn
43. Grappa
44. Lakota
45. Main Street Deli
46. Main Street Pizza & Noodle
47. Mariposa
48. **Mountain Chicken**
49. **Off Main Café**
50. **Pizza Hut**
51. Red Banjo Pizza
52. Sai-Sommet
53. Wasatch Brew Pub
54. **Windy Ridge Café**
55. Wok on Main
56. Zoom

Map 2: Prospector Square and Park Meadows

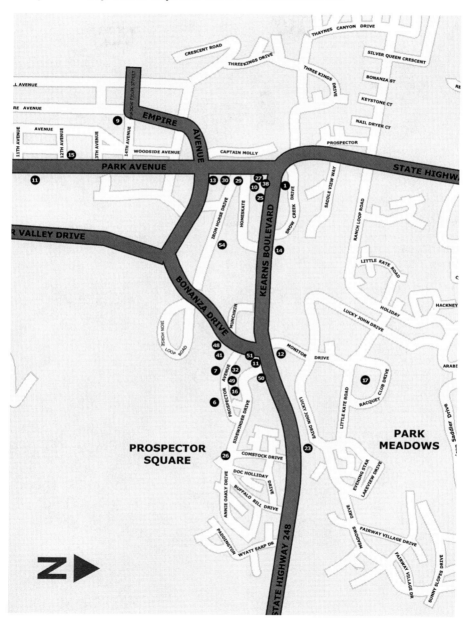